L. GREGORY JONES

CHRISTIAN SOCIAL INNOVATION

Renewing Wesleyan Witness

Abingdon Press
Nashville

CHRISTIAN SOCIAL INNOVATION:
RENEWING WESLEYAN WITNESS

Copyright © 2016 by L. Gregory Jones

Library of Congress Cataloging-in-Publication Data has been requested.

ISBN 978-1-5018-2577-4

16 17 18 19 20 21 22 23 24 25—10 9 8 7 6 5 4 3 2 1
MANUFACTURED IN THE UNITED STATES OF AMERICA

*In honor of my mother and brother, and
in memory of my father*

CONTENTS

PREFACE

This book originated as three lectures delivered to the United Methodist Council of Bishops' Learning Forum in November 2015. I am grateful to Bishop Grant Hagiya for the invitation to deliver these lectures, and I am grateful for the discussions that followed. I also delivered a version of these ideas in early January 2016 at a gathering of Bishop Greg Palmer and his West Ohio Conference Leadership Team. I am grateful to Bishop Palmer and his colleagues for a rich day and a half of conversation about these ideas.

I am also grateful to Brian Milford, the Chief Executive of Abingdon Press, for the invitation to turn those lectures into this book. Brian was a seminary classmate and has been a good friend for more than three decades, and I appreciate his interest in the project without having heard the lectures. Further, since I typically deliver lectures without any notes, Brian committed to this project before seeing anything in writing. That is either a high level of trust or craziness, or perhaps both.

This book reflects the substance of the three lectures, along with an introductory overview and a concluding postscript. I hope the bishops recognize something of what they heard in the broad encouragement for renewing our Wesleyan witness through Christian social innovation. I have written this book in the hope that a broad cross-section of laypeople and clergy, especially younger folks, as well as other church leaders will find encouragement, hope, and stimulation for renewing a Wesleyan witness through Christian social innovation.

This book is a digest of a much larger project on social innovation, leadership, and institutions that my son Nathan Jameson Jones and I have been working on, and that we hope to finish in the near future. Nate has actually been a "contributing author" of this volume because in a number of key places his vision, his voice, and his prose have shaped the argument of this book. The overall perspective of the book has benefited from our joint work and conversations, and I have learned much from him. He also read a draft of this book and offered terrific insights and constructive suggestions.

I am also grateful to my wife, the Reverend Susan Pendleton Jones, our other two children, Ben and Sarah, our daughter-in-law Amy (Nate's wife), and Ben's fiancée, Allison Rhoads. Many of the book's ideas were discussion topics on a fabulous family trip we took in the summer of 2015 to New Zealand and Australia; conversations over meals and on hikes, in airports and on buses and boats, clarified my perspectives and thinking. More recently, Susan and Sarah were enormously valuable in patiently reading multiple drafts of the book, offering wonderful insights, and framing the introductory overview as well as the larger argument of the book.

I am grateful also to friends and colleagues (and two other relatives!) who read an earlier draft of the book and offered prompt feedback: Jason Byassee, Darin Davis, Arthur Jones, Scott Jones, Cate McLeane, Dave Odom, Kavin Rowe, Laceye Warner, and Victoria White. And I am grateful for editing and writing assistance on some of the key points, several years ago, from Ben McNutt and Kelly Gilmer. This book is much stronger and clearer thanks to all of their comments, criticisms, suggestions, and encouragement.

I wish I could blame my family and these friends for any failings that remain. Alas, despite their best efforts to help, any failings in the book are my own. In the true spirit of innovation, I hope I have failed in those places sufficiently quickly that I will be able to succeed sooner in the larger project that this book points toward.

This book, and the larger project, reflect ideas I have been developing and working on throughout my vocation as a pastor, scholar, teacher, and leader. Over the past decade I have focused on developing these ideas in my roles as senior strategist for both leadership education at Duke Divinity and the Fuqua-Coach K Center on Leadership and Ethics at Duke's Fuqua School of Business. I also benefited from conversations with groups from 2012–2015 when I was working alongside the H. E. Butt Family Foundation in Texas, and since 2012 in my work as executive director of A Foundation for Theological Education and its John Wesley Fellows program. I am grateful to these diverse organizations and their leadership for settings to learn and grow and test ideas in conversation.

Thanks also to Morris Williams, a gifted businessman, preacher's son, and longtime supporter of Duke Divinity School and Duke University. I am honored to occupy the chair endowed by Morris and his wife Ruth, a chair focused on the importance of Christian ministry. In the spring of 2015, Morris urged me to focus more time on writing—and writing for a broad audience. His encouragement has been in my mind both in writing this book and as Nate and I work on the larger project. I am grateful for Morris's vision, wisdom, and friendship, and his family's long commitment to the importance of Christian witness for the common good.

The book is dedicated to three people who have most shaped me as a Wesleyan Christian: my father and mother, and my older brother. My father, S. Jameson Jones Jr., was a United Methodist theological educator, pastor, and church leader. He died in 1982, and I still miss hearing his voice, spending time with him, learning from him, and being loved and guided by him.

My mother, Bonnie Jones Shinneman, is a United Methodist diaconal minister, and for much of her life was a church choir director. She also was a leader on the Hymnal Revision Committee that produced the 1989 United Methodist Hymnal, a hymnal that has been enormously influential in helping to renew faithful Wesleyan witness. In addition, she has been a leader of numerous mission trips to Bolivia and the Middle East (especially Beit Sahour), and a Christian social innovator in the development of preschools in both regions.

My brother Scott has been a United Methodist bishop since 2004; he has dedicated his life to scholarship and leadership in the service of renewing Wesleyan witness. I have learned much from his writing, teaching, and leadership, and I am grateful for his lifelong friendship and for ongoing conversations and collaborations with him in service to the gospel.

They, along with my sisters Shelley Rossbach and Jani Tsurumi and my broader extended family, have loved, sustained, and nurtured me in more ways than I can imagine.

In this and all things, to God be the glory.

REDISCOVERING CHRISTIAN SOCIAL INNOVATION

Why Is Innovation So Important?

Most people are hungry for innovation. We are hungry for new ways of living and doing things that can chart better paths forward. We are hungry for innovation because we know that we are facing challenges that are "complex," problems that are "wicked." These words convey that our challenges and problems intersect in ways that make them more difficult to address than just being "complicated" or "hard." Indeed, our challenges and problems intersect so deeply that we need multiple strategies because no single approach can "solve" the challenge or "fix" the problem.

This is true for us in the church, and it is also true for other institutions such as education, health, business, journalism, and civil society itself. It is true for those of us who live in the United States, and it is also true for people living in other parts of the world. Niall Ferguson's provocative book *The Great Degeneration:*

1

How Institutions Decay and Economies Die documents challenges in the Western world: We have a looming sense that too much of our world is in a state of degeneration or disruption, that older institutions and patterns of life are decaying and dying. We have a sense that we need something new.

We are hungry for an approach to innovation that can address what doesn't seem to be working, and also for a model rooted in more organic metaphors of growth, renewal, and vitality. John Gardner pointed toward the importance of innovation for renewal a half-century ago, when in a critique of mechanistic, bureaucratic ways of thinking he wrote,

> Every individual, organization or society must mature, but much depends on how this maturing takes place. A society whose maturing consists simply of acquiring more firmly established ways of doing things is headed for the graveyard—even if it learns to do these things with greater and greater skill. *In the ever-renewing society what matures is a system or framework within which continuous innovation, renewal and rebirth can occur.*[1]

Innovation is a term that includes entrepreneurship, yet is more encompassing. Entrepreneurship, understood as a mindset and practice of starting new ventures, is critically important and to be encouraged. But we also need innovative approaches to renewing existing communities, organizations, and institutions. *Harvard Business Review* describes innovation on its website simply as "the difficult discipline of newness." We are tempted to think that "newness" is just "making stuff up," but to discover newness that is life-giving and sustainable is indeed a difficult discipline.

---

1. John W. Gardner, *Self-Renewal* (New York: Norton, 1963), 5. Italics in the original.

What Is Social Innovation?

Social innovation involves the discovery and development of strategies to build, renew, and transform institutions in order to foster human flourishing. In so doing, it aims at creating a "new equilibrium" that "unleashes new value for society, releases trapped potential, or alleviates suffering."[2] Social innovation, as I use the term, aims at creating social value, and is compatible with a variety of business models (e.g., for-profit, "not-for-profit," or hybrid). Social entrepreneurship is an activity that focuses on starting new initiatives, and is a subset of a larger focus on social innovation.

Greg Dees, a friend and colleague at Duke University, is often referred to as "the father of social entrepreneurship as an academic discipline." His approach to social entrepreneurship embraces the larger horizon of what I describe as social innovation. In 1998, he published a landmark essay, "The Meaning of 'Social Entrepreneurship,'" in which he offered a crisp summary of the work of social entrepreneurs:

Social entrepreneurs play the role of change agents in the social sector by

- adopting a mission to create and sustain social value (not just private value),
- recognizing and relentlessly pursuing new opportunities to serve that mission,

---

2. These two sentences draw on descriptions in two books: David Bornstein and Susan Davis, *Social Entrepreneurship* (New York: Oxford, 2010), 1; and Roger L. Martin and Sally R. Osberg, *Getting Beyond Better: How Social Entrepreneurship Works* (Boston: Harvard Business Review Press, 2015), 10. The quote is from Martin and Osberg.

- engaging in a process of continuous innovation, adaptation, and learning,
- acting boldly without being limited by resources currently in hand, and
- exhibiting heightened accountability to the constituencies served and for the outcomes created.[3]

In reading this list, it struck me: these characteristics describe the Wesleyan revival in eighteenth-century England and the vitality of Wesleyan movements in the nineteenth and early twentieth centuries in the United States and, more recently, in other parts of the world (especially Africa). Even more, these characteristics describe most Christian renewal movements throughout the history of the Church. This comparison led me to the rediscovery of a Christian vision of social innovation.

What Is Christian Social Innovation, Why Does It Matter, and How Does Faith Animate It?

Christian social innovation involves bringing the rich resources of the Christian faith to bear on the mindsets, practices, and traits of social innovation. Indeed, it also entails recovering the close connections between the vitality of Christian witness through the centuries, including my own Wesleyan tradition, and the admirable goals of practitioners and theorists of social innovation and entrepreneurship.

---

3. Greg Dees, "The Meaning of Social Entrepreneurship," October 31, 1998, https://entrepreneurship.duke.edu/news-item/the-meaning-of-social-entrepreneurship/.

"What happened to the Church?" Greg Dees asked me one day over lunch.

It was a reasonable question to the dean of Duke Divinity School. Even so, I was taken aback, unsure of what he was really concerned about. "Could you say a little more about what you are asking?" I responded.

Dees explained, "I am curious why the Church lost interest in entrepreneurial approaches to social needs and problems. For most of American history, faith-based communities led the way in innovative approaches in sectors such as education, health, housing, food, just to name a few. This was particularly true when you think about approaches that achieved scale and scope: faith-based hospitals and hospices, colleges and universities founded by Christians, organizations such as Salvation Army, Habitat for Humanity, and World Vision.

"Yet it seems that about forty to fifty years ago, faith-based communities lost interest in what we now call social entrepreneurship. The field I am now associated with, social entrepreneurship, emerged in business schools in part because of the decline of interest by the Church. And so I wonder, what happened to the Church?"

His question continues to haunt me because his description of the spirit of earlier generations of Christians includes so many of my own forebears, not only Christians in general from the second century onward but Wesleyans in particular since the eighteenth century. The Wesleyan movement, originally in England and then in the United States, and increasingly around the globe, has for much of our history been a leader in social innovation and entrepreneurship.

Wesleyan Christians founded many of our leading colleges and universities in the United States: fine liberal arts colleges as well as research universities across the country such as Boston University, Syracuse, Northwestern, Duke, Vanderbilt, Emory, Southern Methodist University, the University of Denver, and the University of Southern California.

Major initiatives in health care were started by Wesleyan Christians, too. In many states, influential hospital systems bearing the name *Methodist* stand alongside other hospitals founded by other Christian communities such as Baptists, Lutherans, Presbyterians, Episcopalians, and Roman Catholics. In addition, initiatives like the Salvation Army and Goodwill Industries had their origins and inspiration in a Wesleyan vision of Christian witness.

For most of my life, interest in social innovation has been a part of my outlook as a Wesleyan Christian. I found Dees's question disturbing because, in twenty-first-century America, interest in entrepreneurship is primarily a secular phenomenon. Entrepreneurship and innovation are all the rage in popular culture, business schools, and even among some politicians. Start-ups are generating new jobs, creating wealth, and providing solutions to longstanding problems. People are also aware that old-line social institutions need innovative approaches that provide renewal, reestablish trust, increase impact, enhance effectiveness, and cultivate sustainability.

Yet the Church seems disinterested either in the topic or, more importantly, in practicing social entrepreneurship as it is now being described. The burgeoning literature about social entrepreneurship barely mentions the Church or other faith-based institutions, and when it does they are often described as part of the broken institutional landscape.

Roger Martin and Sally Osberg distinguish social **entrepreneurship** from social **advocacy** and social **service**, and they observe that social entrepreneurship takes direct action *and* seeks to transform existing systems. Martin and Osberg note that faith communities are good at social advocacy and social service, but they assume churches have little role in social entrepreneurship.[4]

In recent years, much of the most innovative and entrepreneurial work in the social sector has been done apart from faith communities, whether through secular nongovernmental organizations (e.g., Teach for America, KIPP) or for-profit businesses (e.g., hospitals and hospices). Indeed, it is now often assumed that faith communities are irrelevant to social innovation and entrepreneurship or are a significant obstacle to it.

What happened to the Church? In part, we have forgotten who we are. We have forgotten the story of God's love and redemption, and have too often lived as "practical atheists" who have the form of faith, but little of the substance.[5] A United Methodist bishop asked the leaders of a struggling congregation what differentiated them from the town's Rotary Club. The question stumped the leaders. The bishop left thinking that the difference was that the Rotary Club was more actively engaged in the

---

4. See Martin and Osberg, *Getting Beyond Better*, 8–9, 37. Writing from within the Christian community, Robert D. Lupton has focused on the ways in which Christian "mission" and "charity," especially in the United States, has been operating with impoverished notions of advocacy and service. He begins his recent book *Charity Detox* (New York: HarperOne, 2015) by observing that you cannot "serve others out of poverty." He urges Christians to collaborate with entrepreneurs (Christian and otherwise) to create new organizations that generate new and better jobs for people. See also his earlier book *Toxic Charity* (New York: HarperOne, 2012).

5. "Practical atheism" is a phrase used by John Wesley in his sermon "On Living Without God in the World." It was popularized in the 1980s by Stanley Hauerwas and Will Willimon to characterize the plight of many American congregations.

community, had higher expectations of its members, and has a more coherent story of why it exists.

Secondly, as the Church we also have turned inward and been shaped more by fear than by hope. We have become preoccupied with managing what already exists, rather than focusing on innovative renewal of organizations and entrepreneurial approaches to starting new ones. We have developed bad models and understandings of organizations, relying on images that suggest they are machines rather than organisms.

In addition, we have become accommodated to cultural assumptions. Somewhere along the line, we became content with assuming that people could learn what it means to think and live as a Christian simply by growing up as a good person. For a longer period of time, this was less true of African-American, immigrant, and blue-collar Christians in the United States, who were more acutely aware of the sharp gaps between mainstream American culture and their own social and economic contexts. But even in those communities, there is now less attention to forming Christians than there ought to be.

It is crucial for the Church's own internal integrity and witness that we rediscover a vision for social innovation and entrepreneurship. We need to recover this witness not so we might be relevant, but rather as an intrinsic part of our witness to the God who we believe is making all things new by the power of the Holy Spirit. Ironically, the best way we can become relevant is not by focusing on how to be relevant, but rather by rediscovering and renewing our own mission and purpose.

The social entrepreneurship movement also needs the robust practices and commitments to social innovation offered by faith communities. I began to see this more clearly in a conversation with Greg Dees shortly before he died unexpectedly in 2013. Even though he was not a practicing Christian, he wanted to team-teach a course on social entrepreneurship with me in which faith-based ideas would be central to the course. When I asked him why that was important, he said that unless faith communities once again became integral to social entrepreneurship, the movement itself might run out of steam.

Why did he think faith communities were important to social entrepreneurship? I suspect he was worried in part that social entrepreneurship may depend too much on an assumption that human beings alone can fix everything. The very term *entrepreneurship*, as Dees wrote in his definitive essay, connotes that we are the agents and catalysts who effect significant change and add significant value, typically by starting new things. There is something crucial and powerful in that catalytic activity. Yet faith communities have typically understood human activity to be responsive to God's prior action, thus emphasizing that we are called to be catalytic witnesses to, and participants in, God's work.

Why does that matter? A focus on God's priority enables perseverance in the face of the inevitable frustrations and resistance that we encounter in addressing formidable, often "wicked," problems. Hard problems, like calculus, can be solved if we just roll up our sleeves, work hard, and are persistent. Wicked problems, though, the kind that create the most perplexing and challenging issues, are not solvable just by hard work. Wicked problems typically have multiple dimensions, so that if you work on only one aspect of the problem, it creates new problems in other aspects. And frequently those who are working on the problem are also, often unwittingly, contributing to its wickedness.

9

We need innovative experiments that can help find generative solutions to those wicked problems, coming at things from different and often surprising angles. For example, some research in central Africa indicates that the best way to ensure healthy children at age five is to focus less on medicines and vaccines and more on the education of mothers. The more educated the mother, the more likely the child will benefit in multiple ways. By contrast, when we focus only on medicines and vaccines, we often have difficulties with compliance *and* we discover that there are misaligned incentives in the community.

Creative experiments that explore the multiple dimensions of an issue, such as educating mothers as an initiative in children's health care, offer generative solutions to wicked problems. Attentiveness to God's overarching purposes keeps us focused on the interdependencies of wicked problems and enables us to persevere when we are unable to "fix" things in the short-term.

I suspect that Greg Dees also worried social entrepreneurship may rest on a hollowed-out set of commitments that need to be fortified by a deeper understanding of human nature and flourishing. For example, a Christian vision for social innovation, at its best, depends on a conception of hope that is different from the optimism that often characterizes secular endeavors, a hope that acknowledges personal, social, and systemic brokenness.

Faith communities, at our best, have embodied and continue to embody perseverance, often bringing people together across generations and diverse sectors to imagine how common effort and faith might overcome obstacles. At our best we combine responsiveness to God's prior action and a commitment to hope such that we are resilient and persistent witnesses to a new and *renewed* future.

Although some faith communities have lost the "at our best" focus, new conversations and experiments are emerging beyond the goal of starting new congregations. But they tend to be "and" conversations: faith *and* innovation, faith *and* entrepreneurship, faith *and* leadership.

This doesn't go deep enough. The "and" leaves each of the terms unquestioned, and then explorations begin about whether there might be connections. Dees alluded to how and why faith might truly "animate" social innovation. In this perspective, faith is not held at a distance from the activities of life but is instead its vital force, providing the imagination, passion, and commitment that leads to transformation.

To say that faith animates social innovation (or anything else) suggests something richer and more challenging: faith is not just one more thing—faith is *the* thing. In this way, faith inspires, directs, and works in and through our lives.

Through the centuries, Christian faith has animated social innovation in diverse ways. A key reason for the spread of Christianity in the early centuries of the common era is what my colleague Kavin Rowe calls "Christianity's surprise": its innovative witness in caring for widows, orphans, and the poor. Christians developed the first hospitals and, in the early modern era, Christian congregations pioneered care for those who were mentally ill.

There are also signs of renewed witness to Christian social innovation in the United States, often inspired by our brothers and sisters in other parts of the world: neighborhood clinics, faith-based schools, start-ups to improve opportunities for day-laborers, and renewed missional focus among established organizations.

Greg Dees worried that social entrepreneurship might not endure, much less flourish, unless it reconnects with faith communities. I worry that faith-based organizations, including churches, might not endure, much less flourish, unless they reconnect with social entrepreneurship mindsets, skills, and virtues.

What would it mean, both for faith communities and broader social ecologies, if we recovered life-giving convictions and transformational practices—if faith were to animate social innovation?

I am not suggesting that only people of faith can "truly" practice social innovation, nor even that people of faith are likely to be more "effective." I am suggesting, however, that a Christian vision can and should offer crucial conceptual categories and mindsets as well as exemplary practices—both historical and contemporary—that shed light on the admirable passions, practices, and aspirations of social innovators and entrepreneurs regardless of whether they have any interest in, or connection to, Christian faith.[6]

What Are the Key Markers of Christian Social Innovation?

Christian social innovation, like social entrepreneurship, is passionate about cultivating human ingenuity, nurturing processes that support new and renewed institutions for human flourishing, and creating environments for people and communities to thrive. But in addition to these similarities, there are important differences as well.

Christian social innovation recognizes that it will take more than human ingenuity to solve intractable problems; it will take a

---

6. The clearer we are about how Christian faith "animates" social innovation, we will then be in better position to enter into "and" conversations with those from other perspectives about overlaps and divergences in approaches to social innovation. But we need greater clarity about what we mean by Christian social innovation in order to enter those conversations well.

comprehensive vision of God and the nature and purpose of the world and of human life within it. That vision will also require us to give an account both of the goodness that inspires passion and ingenuity as well as the persistent brokenness (personal as well as systemic sin) that frustrates and often undermines our attempts to provide breakthrough solutions.

Christian social innovation describes a way of life in relationship with God that focuses on building and transforming institutions that nurture generative solutions to wicked social problems, and is shaped by intersections of mindsets and practices of blessing, hope, forgiveness, friendship, imagination, and improvisation. These mindsets and practices are crucial to holding together both the positive commitments that inspire and sustain social innovation and the realistic understandings that often lead to cynicism and despair. And, while they can be distinguished as ideas, they are deeply interrelated in a Christian way of life.

- BLESSING: God's blessing shapes the creation of the world and the vision for its fulfillment. In Genesis, the word *blessing* is introduced when living, breathing creatures are created. God declares the creation good and calls forth the good from all that God blesses, even as brokenness is never far away and awaits healing. Human beings are called to bless God, expressed especially in the final five psalms in a crescendo of praise, and to extend that blessing to all those whom we encounter. The vision of God's reign in its fullness involves blessing (Revelation 22) that is described in the present in the beatitudes of the Sermon on the Mount. Blessing is a way of life lived before the God who first blessed, and continues to bless, humanity and the whole creation.
- HOPE: Hope is the Christian virtue that holds together a positive vision of the future and a realistic assessment

of the present. Positive psychology has emphasized the importance of "learned optimism," and this has spread to other contexts such as "positive organizational behavior." There is much to be said for this emphasis on optimism. Research shows that optimists do better in school, are more successful at work, and live longer and healthier lives. But they often do so by ignoring or distorting key aspects of reality. Research has shows that pessimists see the world more accurately. Christian hope focuses on the positive, rooted in a vision of God and God's reign and the blessing of our created goodness; yet it also is vigilant in attending to the realities of human sin and brokenness.

- FORGIVENESS: God's love takes the form of forgiveness in the wake of sin and evil; it offers a future not bound by the brokenness of the past. This forgiveness means we do not need to be trapped in cycles of vengeance, cynicism, and despair but can be freed for new life and innovation. The gift of forgiveness is a blessing that enables hope to be sustained. Simultaneously, living into an innovative future helps us discover the forgiveness, and the healing of the past, that we need to preserve the best of where we have been. Forgiveness and innovation are linked in ways that hold together the future and the past in a life-giving, blessing, and transforming present.
- FRIENDSHIP: One blessing from God is that we are created for relationship—with God and with others. Human beings flourish in relationship, and forgiveness is essential to friendship with God and with others. Friendship also incubates innovation, because "holy friends" challenge the sins we have come to love, affirm gifts we are afraid to claim, and help us dream dreams we otherwise wouldn't have dreamed. This gift of friendship enables us to discover forgiveness and to imagine together an audacious future shaped by God's love for the world.

14

- IMAGINATION: We are called and invited to see the world as God does. This means seeing it through the lens of blessing, hope, forgiveness, and friendship, seeing the possibilities for human flourishing and for the flourishing of all creation. This call requires an ongoing process of unlearning our default assumptions that reflect sin and brokenness, and learning to imagine the world's purpose, our own vocations, and our communities' and institutions' vision and mission in the light of God. Ephesians 3:20-21 calls us to dream God's dreams in extraordinary ways that transform our limited human capacities: "Glory to God, who is able to do far beyond all that we could ask or imagine by his power at work within us; glory to him in the church and in Christ Jesus for all generations, forever and always. Amen" (CEB).

- IMPROVISATION: We can and should experiment with innovative solutions because the final end of God's reign is in God's hands rather than ours. We are called to responsible action rooted in hope that seeks to bear witness to the goodness of God and God's blessing and improves the world in which we live, and we are freed from the burden of thinking that it is all up to our ingenuity. Further, improvisation is not about innovation understood as "making stuff up" from scratch; rather, it is about drawing on the best of the past, and discerning the gifts around us, in a "yes, and" culture that builds bridges rather than fosters opposition.

The intersections of these themes are illumined in the story of Jesus's feeding of the five thousand. Jesus offers an innovative solution to a practical problem: too many people and too little food. He offers a pattern that becomes a paradigm of the hospitality for Christian life: "take, bless, break, and give." What people would otherwise have thought was a problem of scarcity becomes instead an opportunity to reveal God's abundance.

In stories such as these, we discover freedom for innovation: learning forgiveness and hope in the blessing offered by God in Christ in the wake of our own and the world's brokenness; being invited into renewed friendship with God and others, we then are called to respond imaginatively and improvisationally in our witness in the world.

At our best, Wesleyans have offered a distinctive vision of Christian life at these intersections and have fostered remarkable social innovation. Wesleyans have had in our DNA a commitment to integrative thinking that holds together ideas and practices that others have tended to make oppositional (e.g., tradition and innovation, personal and social holiness, small groups and the sacraments, belief in Christian perfection and acknowledgment of the pervasiveness of sin, grace and works, evangelism and social justice, personal salvation and organizational zeal, intellect/reason and emotions/feelings).

This is only to say that a commitment to Christian social innovation is a Wesleyan distinctive, not that it is exclusive to Wesleyans or to be defined over-against other traditions. Many other Christian traditions exemplify the richness of Christian social innovation and, in the cases of Roman Catholicism and Eastern Orthodoxy, for a much longer history, on a broader scale, and often with great effectiveness. Much can be learned from exemplary insights and practices from other traditions, as well as from other religious and secular perspectives. Yet we Wesleyans ought not hide our light under a bushel, for in the Wesleyan movements around the world we have borne a distinctive witness to Christian social innovation in transformative, life-giving ways.

At our worst, though, we have forgotten who (and whose) we are, where we are headed, and whence we have come. We have turned inward and become bureaucratic, and we have accommodated to the worst patterns of the cultures in which we find ourselves. We have not only hid our light under a bushel; at times we have forgotten that there is a light at all.

In order to bear witness to the light, we need to recapture our part in God's story, and recognize that the End is our beginning (chapter 1). We need to rediscover an outward orientation that enables us to practice traditioned innovation (chapter 2). And we need to discover afresh that the best way to serve the cultures in which we live is through intensive formation of communities of character that bear witness to God's reign (chapter 3). My focus in this book is primarily on the "why" and the "what" of Christian social innovation; more attention to the "how" is the task of another project.

One of the most compelling witnesses to the light is Maggy Barankitse, a remarkable Christian social innovator from Burundi (in central Africa) whose story I describe more fully in chapter 2. She told me once that she prays the same, simple prayer every morning, wherever she is. She typically prays it in Kirundi, her native language, or perhaps in French, her second language. An English translation of the prayer goes like this:

Lord, let your miracles break forth every day,
and let me not be an obstacle in any way.

This prayer gets at the heart of why a Christian vision of social innovation is so distinctive, and also so crucial. It is shaped by a conviction that God continues to produce miracles, reminding us that whatever vision and passion and commitment we bring to our hopes for transformation, God's work precedes and transcends our own ingenuity. Such a belief in miracles inspires a sense of blessing, hope, forgiveness, friendship, imagination, and improvisation. And it is equally shaped by an awareness of our own capacity for sin, and others' also, in a way that leads to self-awareness, a focus on God. Thus amazing dreams that can be accomplished, even here, even now, even by you and me and networks of others praying and innovating together.

In order to see more clearly how and why we are called to Christian social innovation, we need to rediscover the story that shapes who we are and are called to be. We need to learn again why the End is our beginning.

Chapter 1

THE END IS OUR BEGINNING

Living with a Clear Sense of Purpose

Framing the Perspective

Many people know what they do, and even how they do it. Perhaps even more feel confident in who (and whose) they are. Christian social innovation depends on a clear and driving sense of purpose—the *why*.

Simon Sinek delivered a TED talk in 2009 that has been viewed more than twenty-five million times. It is called "Start with Why." He contends that most people and most organizations start with a rational explanation of what they do and how they do it. People are typically very clear about what they do, and often somewhat clear about how they do it. But they tend to be fuzziest about why they do what they do. The best leaders and organizations, Sinek argues, reverse that order: they are clearest about their purpose, their why, and that leads them to explain how they accomplish their purpose and what they do to further those accomplishments. The most innovative breakthroughs come from people and organizations that start with why.

Christian social innovation offers a distinctive vision of social innovation because, at our best, Christians have a very clear sense of purpose: to bear witness to the reign of God that was announced and embodied in Jesus Christ and is present now through the work of the Holy Spirit who is making all things new. Can you imagine a better rationale or a more comprehensive sense of purpose?

We actually should expect to see extraordinary Christian social innovation in the world, and should be surprised when we see unimaginative Christians. Sinek himself points to Martin Luther King Jr.'s speech on the mall in Washington, DC, on August 28, 1963: 250,000 people showed up, less to hear a famous black preacher speak, and more because King was giving voice to a vision that expressed their own longings. They wanted to see a more hopeful, a more just, a more forgiving world come into being. And, as Sinek notes, King gave voice to that by saying "I have a dream"—not "I have a plan."

King was bearing witness to the Christian dream of a transformed creation, to an extraordinary imagination for God's reign and a plea that it would come in its fullness: a vision of when, as Revelation 21:1-5a illumines, "a new heaven and a new earth" appears where God will "wipe away every tear" from our eyes, a time when "death will be no more...no mourning, crying, or pain anymore, for the former things have passed away." King drew on the prophetic imagination of Amos 5, and traditions of black preachers evoking a time when young black children and young white children would walk hand in hand together. It wasn't so much that King had a dream that he developed on his own; he was recalling for millions of Americans a dream they had already glimpsed in stories about God and God's love. King articulated that dream in ways deeply resonant with people's longings.

King's dream of a transformed future recalls a beautiful prayer in Ephesians 3:18-21. The writer prays that we may "have the power to grasp love's width and length, height and depth, together with all believers" so that we will "be filled entirely with the fullness of God." The prayer concludes with these powerful words: "Glory to God, who is able to do far beyond all that we could ask or imagine by his power at work within us; glory to him in the church and in Christ Jesus for all generations, forever and always. Amen."

If we are oriented toward the goal of comprehending, with our whole life—thoughts, emotions, perceptions, and actions—the fullness of God's work in Christ by the power of the Spirit, we are set on fire to dream extraordinary dreams for the world, ourselves, and our communities and institutions. God's power at work within us is able to accomplish "abundantly far more than all we can ask or imagine" (Eph 3:20-21 NRSV). I don't know about you, but I'd settle for God being able to accomplish *all* I could ask or imagine. But the End of God's reign goes well beyond that: Ephesians wants to stretch our imaginations to envision as much as possible of what God is doing—*far beyond* all I could ask or imagine—and to live into that vision improvisationally.

In so doing, we discover a beginning for social innovation rooted in a profound sense of hope. To be sure, we discover a *new* beginning, because we discover our need for forgiveness that can heal the brokenness of the past for the sake of transformed life in the future. That new beginning helps us also live into new forms of friendship with God and with others, where we discover that, as King put it, the content of our character matters far more than does the color of our skin or, we might add, any of the other markers that divide us from each other and lead us to violence, despair, or sometimes, just a cold indifference. We discover the power of the Holy Spirit who is making all things new.

Rediscovering Wesleyan Witness and Scriptural Imagination

The Wesleyan movement developed its momentum in eighteenth-century England by discovering the End as its new beginning. The early "Methodists," as followers of John and Charles Wesley came to be called, were people who anticipated God's reign. They were focused on the power of the Holy Spirit to nurture new life in people, churches, and other institutions.

The only requirement for joining one of the Wesleyan gatherings in eighteenth-century England was "a desire to flee the wrath to come, and to be saved from their sins." This language still exists as a part of United Methodist doctrine, indeed constitutionally protected doctrine, in *The Discipline* under "The General Rules." The Wesleys did not create a list of requirements to become a part of the movement; they invited anyone who desired salvation with a focus on God's reign. Their invitation came as a form of blessing to people looking for signs of new life, even while knowing that the reality of sin and evil persisted.

The Wesleys were aware, though, of the importance of unlearning old habits of sin and brokenness and learning a new way of life. In this, they were people of hope. The Wesleys focused their teaching on the positive potential of human beings having been redeemed by Christ: the significance of "Christian perfection" as the goal of Christian life. But they were also acutely aware of the power of sin in human life, and expected people to gather in "class meetings" and "bands" every week to unlearn sin and learn holiness of heart and life. Forgiveness and friendship were crucial in shaping faithful Christian life and imagination (see more in chapter 3).

The Wesleys' focus on the End also led them to be imaginative and improvisational in renewing Christian community and developing new Christian institutions. Their "societies" were an innovation on the early Christian catechumenate and its focus on forming Christians.[1]

Further, the Wesleys developed and encouraged experiments in such areas as education (especially the Kingswood School), publishing, health care, economic development, and prison reform. They recognized that new institutions were important in bearing witness to the good news of God's love in Christ empowered by the Holy Spirit *and* to combating forces of sin and evil in the world.

A historian of the Methodist experience in America writing in the middle decades of the twentieth century entitled his study *Organizing to Beat the Devil.*[2] At our best, Wesleyan Christians have been inspired to create and renovate institutions because of our passionate commitment to the End. Something crucial has been at stake. Inspired by a confidence in the triumph of God's reign, and a persistent awareness of the reality of sin and evil,

---

1. See John Wesley's description in "A Plain Account of the People Called Methodists," Section I, Paragraph 10.

2. Charles W. Ferguson, *Organizing to Beat the Devil: Methodists and the Making of America* (New York: Doubleday, 1971).

American Methodists in the nineteenth and early twentieth centuries practiced Christian social innovation in quite remarkable ways.

Yet, in recent decades American Methodists, at least in those forms that reflect a primarily Anglo and established character, have lost much of our commitment to social innovation. A large part of our predicament is that we have lost our sense of the End. We have become preoccupied with the "what" and the "how" and have lost the power of "why": we have lost sight of the End.

Why have we lost our vision of the End? In part, we have done so because we inhabit the modern Western world, where in the latter part of the twentieth century and the early decades of the twenty-first we have assumed that we live in what philosopher Charles Taylor called "a secular age."[3] Unlike the Wesleys (and most of our Christian forebears), current dominant Western assumptions take for granted that anything and everything can be explained without recourse to God. Ironically, Taylor suggests, even Christians tend to assume this.

This influential cultural trend has been intensified for establishment United Methodists. Over the last century, we increasingly identified ourselves with established cultural norms and thus didn't feel like we still had to ask ourselves about the "why" of our mission and purpose; we took it for granted. We were the denomination of established America.

We became preoccupied with questions of what and how without any awareness of the why. A contemporary commentator on our current plight might suggest that United Methodists are

---

3. See Charles Taylor, *A Secular Age* (Cambridge, MA: Harvard University Press, 2007). An accessible and insightful summary of the main themes of Taylor's argument is found in James K. A. Smith, *How (Not) to be Secular: Reading Charles Taylor* (Grand Rapids, MI: Eerdmans, 2014).

no longer organizing to beat the devil but rather organizing for the sake of organizing—a great definition of bureaucracy!

We now think and act as if we can restructure and reorganize ourselves into renewal. We complain about our lack of growth, we long for better leaders, and we develop nostalgia for the good old days. We cling to old-style methods of social advocacy and social service rather than having an identity and mission that would lead us to a new beginning: Christian social innovation shaped by the End.

While contemporary United Methodism needs to rediscover Wesleyan renewal, we also need to recognize that losing sight of the End is a recurring temptation for all of us in a fallen world. The challenge of discovering that the End is our beginning is one that not only United Methodism faces, nor only that Westerners face in a secular age: it is a recurring temptation that we all face in a world that continues to be marred by sin and brokenness.

The ancient Israelites faced this temptation to lose sight of the End and become preoccupied with survival in ways that divided people from each other when they were in the wilderness after the Exodus. The story is told in the book of Numbers.

At some point for the Israelites in the wilderness, it all became unhinged. There, in the wilderness, pain and suffering tore away the communal bonds that made endurance possible. The cumulative effect of the general conditions bears some blame, too, for the deterioration. Traveling miles on sand and rock, especially in the sweltering heat, can break even the strongest wills. These and the other devices of land and weather slowly carved themselves into the people, as if nature were some evil sculptor bent on a masterpiece. It chipped away a little, and then more, until a slight crevice ran down Israel's spine. A single doubt about what had caused their predicament turned into a single complaint; and complaining soon became Israel's norm.

Then the resources went. There was a little less to go around at mealtimes. The water sources diminished and became more brackish. The cattle thinned and so did the children's faces. It wasn't the first time they had had to go without, but it followed a long line of agonies—some great, some small—and all forming a gradual dissatisfaction with both the circumstances and with those who led them there.

At the edge of their destination, the complaints increased, the divisions intensified; the cracks in their collective identity and purpose grew deeper and more pronounced. They reached that internal limit where ultimate hope and purpose are overrun by the demands of daily survival. Such demands create a bitterness that requires the kind of satisfaction only a scapegoat can provide: "Why have you brought us into the desert to die, Moses?"

In the Hebrew biblical tradition, this book of the Bible is known as "In the Wilderness." Greek translators, noting the two censuses taken of the people of Israel (the first in chapter 1 and the second in chapter 26), called it "Arithmoi'" and the Latinists, "Numeri," until translation sucked the last bit of ancient whimsy from the name, leaving English-speakers with the rather uninspiring designation we have today: Numbers.

The name "Numbers" was not intended to stoke the fires of the imagination. No doubt few of us (if any) have wandered in the desert southeast of Palestine, either. But all of us know something about being "in the wilderness," of feeling lost or overwhelmed by the necessities of survival to the extent that we can't even lift our eyes to heaven, or recall the hope and purpose that anchors our identity. "In the Wilderness" communicates so much more than "Numbers." Being in the wilderness—an ancient or modern one—is a time of chaos, instability, uncertainty. We lose our way in the wilderness. We don't know where we're going or why we're going there. We lose sight of who we are and whose we are. That's Israel's situation in the story, and it's our situation today.

At God's calling, the Israelites follow Moses out of Egypt, through an inhospitable wilderness and toward the promise of an unseen land. When we meet them at the beginning of Numbers, they're tired and desperate, confused and annoyed. They're beginning to wonder why they left Egypt. Stuck in the wilderness, Israel faces a crisis of vision and leadership that forces them to come to terms with their identity and purpose as a people called by God.

In the midst of crisis Israel does what any modern-day career counselor tells a person who loses a job: get a routine. In the first ten chapters, there's the opening census when they take stock of themselves and try to get organized. They arrange how the tribes should relate to each other and what roles each tribe should have within Israel's collective life. They receive instructions for and attend to the construction of the Meeting Tent and its priestly functions. Among the debilitating chaos of the wilderness, Israel attempts to provide an order to its collective life.

In modern terms, we would call this "institution building." But Israel shows us that institution building is more than simple organizational management for the sake of bureaucratic efficiency. The census, the Meeting Tent instructions, the different roles of Israel's tribes and the rules they follow—together they are the structural embodiment of what it means to be Israel, to be a people made holy, to be a blessing to the world and a witness to Yahweh's reign. Institution building isn't a necessary evil; it is integral to their identity as a people; it is the structural pattern of who they are, and a sign of blessing. To be Israel means to be organized in just this way. Institution building is identity building.

Organized as they are, they face a crisis, and one that has a narrative pattern. David Stubbs, in his insightful commentary on Numbers, notices an *X*-like structure to the story (what biblical scholars call a chiastic structure) that begins in chapter 11, extends through chapter 21, and centers on the story of Moses sending out the twelve spies to scope out the land promised to Israel by Yahweh.[4]

```
A (11:1-3)
Complaints
            B (11:4-34)
            Food
                        C (11:35–12:16)
                        Leadership
                                    D (13:1–14:45)
                                    Promised Land
                        C' (16:1–17:11)
                        Leadership
            B' (20:2-13)
            Water
A' (21:4-9)
Complaints
```

The narrative structure looks like this: In both 11:1-3 (A) and 21:4-9 (A-prime) Israel suffers misfortunes that lead to whining of a general sort. Preoccupied with themselves in destructive ways, the complaining intensifies in 11:4-34 (B) and 20:2-13 (B-prime) from general complaints to grumbling about necessities like food

---

4. Adapted from David L. Stubbs, *Numbers* (Grand Rapids, MI: Brazos, 2009), 113.

and water. In effect, Israel is saying, "We're stuck in the wilderness and we don't have the means to sustain ourselves."

Then, in chapters 11:35–12:16 (C) and in chapters 16:1–17:11 (C-prime), the complaints focus on Israel's leadership. Envy surfaces. First, Miriam's and Aaron's complaints amount to "Why does Moses get to be the leader? We don't like what he's calling us to do." The narrator indicates God's answer: "Because Moses is humble." In fact, "he's more humble than any other person on the face of the earth." Humble? The Bible's portrayal of Moses doesn't exactly suggest humility as his dominant character trait. As Richard Briggs shows in *The Virtuous Reader*, the paradox present in Numbers is analogous to an old country-western song that goes, "Oh Lord it's hard to be humble / when you're perfect in every way." But Briggs also suggests that the humility of Moses doesn't stem from a false sense of his own abilities. Moses's humility doesn't align with our tendency to correlate humility with self-deprecation or self-effacement, passivity or indecision. In contrast, the story's narrator presents Moses as humble because he's intimate with God. God calls Moses humble because Moses possesses the kind of divine intimacy that makes him realize that he's not God. The further he's drawn into intimacy with God, the more he realizes the extent of the difference between himself and God. And that's tremendously humbling. Complaints about Moses's leadership in chapter 12 (C) rebound in chapter 16 (C-prime) but to a degree that threatens the very unity of Israel. Rebellion breaks out, led by Korah son of Izhar. He gathers 250 Israelites for his cause—many from his tribe, the Levites, who had already played a significant role in Israel's life. They set themselves against Moses, and this time, Aaron as well. Moses seems to have reached his own breaking point. Quite put out by Korah and the other Levites, Moses can't understand their grab for more power when Yahweh has already entrusted them to be the priests of Israel. There's a certain dramatic irony to this moment in the story; 16:9 echoes 12:3 but in the form of a rebuke: "Isn't it enough for you that Israel's God has separated you from the Israelite community to allow you to approach him, to perform the service of the Lord's dwelling, and to serve before the community by ministering for them?" Whereas Moses finds humility in his intimate relationship with God, the Levites find an opportunity to jockey for more power. The infighting and division eventually leads to the death of Korah and his 250 followers, a punishment that Moses himself tries to prevent.

To summarize: after Israel's misfortunes and complaints (A and A-prime) lead to more intense complaints about food and water (B and B-prime), which then lead them to then call into question Moses's leadership (C and C-prime), the chiastic structure comes to its center (D), at the point in the narrative (13:1–14:45) where Moses sends the twelve spies to survey the promised land.

The spies behave like present-day American Methodists, because when they return, they have a majority report and a minority report. The majority, ten of the twelve spies, report back, *Oh, it's a land flowing with milk and honey, but we can't go there because there are so many obstacles. There are creatures out there that look like giants, and we look like grasshoppers. We'd better go back to Egypt.*

Only two of the twelve, Joshua and Caleb, say, *Yes, it's a land flowing with milk and honey and we can trust God that God will lead us to the promised land.* Notice that they don't deny the reality of the situation. Joshua and Caleb don't come back to the Israelites and say, *Oh there aren't any obstacles up ahead. We've got this.*

No problem. They simply say, *We can trust that God will lead us there.* At this pivotal point of the journey and its hardships, at the border of the promise, this last circumstance proved too much. They saw the land, but did not understand it. They saw the obstacles but forgot the promise. The people side with the majority report: "Let's go back to Egypt." Why Egypt? Egypt was suffering. Egypt was slavery. Egypt was oppression. But Egypt was *familiar.* Familiarity, especially in times of uncertainty, has a strong pull on the human soul.

My father, who was a United Methodist pastor, used to say that every church he served or was a part of had a "Back to Egypt" committee in it. The truth, however, is even more challenging: each of us has a "Back to Egypt" part of our souls. When faced with being in the wilderness, with uncertainty, with risk, with not knowing where God is leading us, when we don't have a clear sense of direction, we long to return to what is familiar. It's safer that way. We may even see where God is calling us, but we falter once we see the obstacles up ahead. We forget our identity, we forget God's promise, and we even forget our purpose for leaving Egypt in the first place. We see creatures that look like giants; we imagine ourselves as grasshoppers.

In the wilderness, Israel loses sight of what it means to be the people of God on a journey to the promised land. Deeper than the whining and the complaints—deeper even than the issue of leadership—is a crisis of faith, of trust, of hope. The Israelites lose a sense of where they are going and who is guiding them. They forget their "why." The crisis they face in the wilderness is a crisis of identity: they have lost their sense of the End, and so they don't know where to begin.

There is a tinge of irony here. Right on the cusp of their arriving at their *destination*, they lose sight of their *End*, what the Greeks call *telos*—their overarching purpose as God's chosen people. They saw the promised land, but forgot why they were going there and who was guiding them to it. Instead they longed to go back to Egypt.

What happens when we join the "back to Egypt" crowd?

We become bitter rather than focused on blessing. Rather than focusing on the future and the manifold ways in which God blesses the world, and us, we become bitter about our current circumstances and challenges. This bitterness fuels complaints and divisions rather than creative and resilient strategies for bearing witness to God. Living as a blessing, an integral part of Christian social innovation, is not pretending that there is no suffering, that there are no challenges. Nor is it pretending, with the so-called "prosperity gospel" preachers, that God wants believers to become materially wealthy.

To live from the End is to renounce bitterness, complaint, and division for the sake of a focus on the goodness and blessing of God. Such a focus includes lament in the face of suffering, especially unjust suffering, as an integral component of faithful prayer, discernment, and friendship with God. Lament is very different from complaint; the former draws us closer to God and expresses our yearning for God to close the gap between the End and our current experience, whereas the latter causes us to immerse ourselves in misery because it is familiar.

We become crookbacked rather than imaginative. In the sixth century CE, Pope Gregory the Great described the temptation of leaders to get stuck and lose sight of the End in vivid terms:

The crookbacked is one who is weighed down by the burden of earthly cares, so that he never looks up to the things that are above, but is wholly intent on what is underfoot in the lowest sphere. If at any time he hears something good about the heavenly fatherland, he is so weighed down by the burden of evil habit that he does not raise up the face of his heart; he cannot lift up the cast of his thought, being kept bowed down by his habitual earthly solicitude.[5]

When we become overly preoccupied with maintaining the activities of our institutions, when the fear of scarcity overwhelms us, when survival dominates our mindset, we lose sight of God. We're bent over, so focused on the ground that we no longer have a view of heaven—the End of God's reign. We're crookbacked. It's an apt description of Israel in Numbers, of leaders in Pope Gregory's time, and of many of us today. Bent over, weighed down with concerns for survival, we grow forgetful of the God who called us out of Egypt and into the promised land.

We become practical atheists rather than Spirit-inspired people of hope. We focus our attention on earthly things, seek quick fixes, and live as if there is no God. Even Christians today too often live with default mindsets of secularity, rather than believing that God continues to be active in the world guiding us, and the whole creation, toward its promised fulfillment.

The African-American Christian traditions, including their Wesleyan varieties, have done a far better job of staying focused on the power of God. The intensity of the suffering that African Americans have endured has nonetheless sustained and renewed their hope for a new and renewed future given by God. Out of the slumbers of established American culture, including in the

---

5. Pope Gregory the Great, *Pastoral Care*, trans. Henry Davis (New York: Paulist, 1978), 1:41–42.

churches, comes the resounding chorus from the Wesleyan tradition: "We are marching to Zion, beautiful beautiful Zion, we are marching upward to Zion, the beautiful city of God."

The Catholic writer Dorothy Day noted that she wanted to live her life in a way that wouldn't make sense if God doesn't exist. She did so through her powerful witness in the Catholic Worker movement. I confess that too much of my life makes sense without God. And too many of the mindsets and activities of the contemporary Church, especially established United Methodism, makes sense apart from God. Contemporary Christians, including the United Methodist Church, spend too much time going back to Egypt.

Cultivating a Christian Vision for Today

We need to rediscover what it means to see the End as our beginning, to live as witnesses to God's inbreaking reign. People are eager for a sense of purpose for their lives, evidenced by the popularity of Rick Warren's *Purpose Driven* book series. What would rediscovering the End as our beginning involve?

Beginning with the End enables us to discover new beginnings through forgiveness. A focus on the End begins with who God is and what God is doing in the world rather than who we are or what we have done. This leads us to a positive orientation and enables us to see our present and past in a new light. We discover that it is the same Jesus Christ who announces and embodies the inbreaking reign of God who enables us to live into that reign through the forgiveness of the cross and resurrection. Easter provides a new beginning, and a mindset that leads us to focus on the work of the Holy Spirit in making all things new. As a popular

Christian song written by Avery and Marsh puts it, "Every morning is Easter morning, from now on!"

We typically understand forgiveness as redemption of the past so that we can live into a new future. Yet we also discover forgiveness and new beginnings as we learn to live into the new future provided by God. Just as forgiveness can lead to innovation, so focusing on innovation helps us discover forgiveness afresh.

When we are tempted to go back to Egypt, we immerse ourselves in our wounds and so constrain our capacity to imagine, much less live into, the fullness of God's future. Insofar as we lean into the End, and discover again a trust in the character of God's love, goodness, and promises, the more we will discover forgiveness and its accompanying freedom from the burdens of the past.

I learned this from the Amish community in the wake of the horrific school shooting at Nickel Mines, Pennsylvania, in 2006. The Amish offered a powerful witness to the world when they immediately expressed forgiveness for the shooter who had killed five girls, and injured five more, from their community. Five years later, in 2011, I was fortunate to have dinner with some of the families who had lost a daughter, granddaughter, or sister on that tragic day. I listened as they described their roller-coaster journey of coming to terms with their grief and discovering a hope-filled future.

Even as the Amish families were committed to forgiveness, they also were tempted to immerse themselves in the brokenness of the past. By living into the future, and even doing new things such as reaching out to others who suffered tragedies like the families who lost loved ones in the Virginia Tech shooting a year later in 2007, they discovered new depths of forgiveness and thus new beginnings for their own lives. They described the importance of trusting the Holy Spirit as they were guided into an innovative future as a crucial component of discovering forgiveness and healing of the past. They described a deeper and more life-giving relationship with God as a result.[6]

Beginning with the End involves friendship with God, and thus learning to see as God sees. Our journey of learning to see as God sees helps us overcome our desire to go back to Egypt, to immerse ourselves in our wounds, to focus more on survival (the what and the how) rather than our purpose (the why). Forgiveness helps us restore trust, even as our growing trust by living into the future with God helps us discover deeper dimensions of forgiveness.

Beginning with the End invites us into mindsets and practices that nurture friendship with God. Just as our friends influence how we see the world, so friendship with God helps us see things from God's perspective. The letter of James calls Abraham a "friend of God" (James 2:23 NRSV), and Jesus tells his disciples that they are no longer servants but friends (John 15:15). St. Thomas Aquinas describes Christian life as an ever-deepening journey of friendship with God. A focus on Christian life as friendship with God leads us to mindsets of abundance rather than scarcity, hope rather than fear, improvisation rather than survival.[7]

We learn through prayer to comprehend, as Ephesians 3 suggests, the height and depth and length and breadth of Christ. This inspires us to trust that God can indeed accomplish abundantly far more than all we can ask or imagine—though God does this,

---

6. For further reflection on this example, see L. Gregory Jones, "Reconciling Leadership from Nickel Mines," *Faith & Leadership*, October 4, 2011, https://www.faithandleadership.com/l-gregory-jones-reconciling-leadership-nickel-mines.

7. For a beautiful description of Christian life as a journey of friendship with God, see Paul Wadell, *Becoming Friends* (Grand Rapids, MI: Brazos, 2002).

Ephesians suggests, by "working through us." God yearns for us to be shaped by the extraordinary vision of God's reign and to live into that future.

As we engage in Christian practices, we discover a growing intimacy with God that characterizes the humility that God praises in Numbers 12. The God who befriends us in the life, death, and resurrection of Jesus Christ calls us to intimacy with God and to befriending others—especially by showing hospitality to strangers, and so perhaps entertaining "angels without knowing it" (Heb 13:2 CEB), and loving enemies (Matt 5:44). Stanley Hauerwas and Will Willimon describe the friendship Jesus invites us into as "the risky but blessed playground of the Spirit's work."[8]

We are called to overcome our tendency toward violence, vengeance, and division through innovative efforts at reconciliation. For example, when Abraham Lincoln faced criticism for saying kind words about the South, he responded, "Don't I destroy my enemies if I make them my friends?"

St. Paul notes in 2 Corinthians 5 that anyone who is "in Christ" discovers "a new creation" in which the old has passed away and everything has "become new." We are thus called to be "ambassadors" for Christ in bearing witness to the End of the new creation. Serving as an ambassador means that we represent Christ in all that we are and do; we can only do so faithfully as we learn to see as God sees us, the world, our relationships, and the possibilities for new life.

The closer we are to God in intimate friendship, our experience of the present will be more disorienting and we will become more hopeful. The more we see as God sees, the greater the gap

---

8. Stanley Hauerwas and William H. Willimon, *Holy Spirit* (Nashville: Abingdon Press, 2015), 75.

between what can be and what currently is. Focused on the future, we will be attentive to the gaps and inspired to become creative, resilient, and engaged in social innovation.

Beginning with the End nurtures an improvisational spirit. God is the One who created and redeemed the world in Christ, and God will bring creation to its fulfillment in the End. We are freed from the burden of trying to make the world, history, or our own lives turn out right; we are also freed from the despair of thinking that the world is a nightmare with no purpose or meaning. As Sam Wells suggests in his book *Improvisation*, Christians believe the story of our world is a five-act drama: Creation, Israel, Christ, Church, Kingdom. We now live in the fourth act, bearing witness to what God will do in the fifth act. As Wells puts it,

> [Christians] have no need to make everything come right, nor have they need to correct perceived shortcomings in any of the previous three acts. They simply use the resources of the first three acts, and what they anticipate of the final act, and faithfully play with the circumstances in which they find themselves.[9]

Such faithful play can, and should, lead to extraordinary possibilities for social innovation, precisely because our play is oriented toward the abundant beauty and joy of God's reign.

The circumstances in which we find ourselves are often daunting. It is not unusual for us to be bewildered in the wilderness, even to the point of wanting to go back to Egypt. An improvisational spirit will lead us to focus our fear on the Lord, as the psalmist repeatedly encourages, rather than fear of the future. One or another form of "don't be afraid" is the most frequent injunction

---

9. Samuel Wells, *Improvisation* (Grand Rapids, MI: Brazos, 2004), 67.

in all of scripture, appearing more than 350 times, because we often get trapped into mindsets in which our bewilderment leads to the kind of fear that leads to paralysis if not regression. By contrast, "the fear of the Lord"—a focus on the awe and reverence appropriate to a God who brings life out of death, restoration out of exile, joy out of despair—leads us to trust God and lean with improvisation into the future. The psalmist reminds us, "Fear of the LORD is where wisdom begins" (Psalm 111:10 CEB).

Our bewilderment may result less from the wilderness than our disorientation because of the severe gaps between present circumstances and God's intended future. Such gaps give rise to prophetic criticisms in scripture, such as Amos's polemic against Israel's injustice. But prophetic criticism in the Bible is always connected to a vision of the End; it is not disconnected criticism or complaint from bystanders. Prophetic criticism is connected to discovering more faithful ways of living into the future that more closely approximate the End.

Our bewilderment may also result from changes afoot in the broader world. We are living in such an era in the early twenty-first century. Enormous changes are occurring, the result of deep trends, that make us feel like the tectonic plates of culture are shifting beneath us: the digital revolution, closer proximities and engagements among multiple ethnicities and cultures (often called "globalization"), the lure of cities, a growing sense that our institutions are broken.

An improvisational spirit, focused on the End, enables faithful playfulness so that we can overcome our bewilderment by charting new paths forward. We can afford to say "yes, and" to the challenges and opportunities we encounter rather than defining ourselves in opposition with a "no, but" approach. In so doing, we are likely to develop patterns of social innovation that are rooted in breakthrough insights and practices.

Dreaming for Transformation

Beginning with the End, by learning to see as God sees, also orients us toward God's extraordinary future. **Beginning with the End frees us to dream, and to live into those dreams with nimble and effective execution.** Claiming the End as the heart of our story is critical for Christians, and it also raises those "why" questions that all organizations must ask: Why should we exist? What would be lost if we disappeared? What transformational possibilities emerge because of us?

"Make no little plans" wrote the nineteenth-century architect Daniel Burnham. "They have no magic to stir [humanity's] blood and probably themselves will not be realized." Instead,

> Make big plans; aim high in hope and work, remembering that a noble, logical diagram once recorded will never die, but long after we are gone will be a living thing, asserting itself with ever-growing insistency. Remember that our sons and daughters are going to do things that will stagger us. Let your watchword be order and your beacon, beauty. Think big.[10]

Burnham's statement was more than rhetorical; it embodied his commitment to the design of the 1893 World's Fair, the Flat-iron building in New York, and Union Station in Washington, DC. Ideas like these stirred Burnham's blood, inspiring him to translate those big thoughts and dreams into big actions.

10. Burnham, quoted in Charles Moore, *Daniel H. Burnham, Architect, Planner of Cities*, vol. 2 (Boston: Houghton Mifflin, 1921), 147.

Yet Burnham understood it wasn't just about making his ideas happen. His encouragement to "think big" extends beyond the horizon of his own life and legacy. "Remember that our sons and daughters are going to do things that will stagger us," he insists. For him, thinking big is not narcissism disguised as entrepreneurialism but a way of thinking that has others—and investment in others, particularly young people—at its core. Think big, he says, because if you do, you will enable others to flourish by providing possibilities for younger generations to do astounding, life-giving work in the future.

Burnham's remarks on the importance of "thinking big" call to mind the astonishing history of the Methodist Hospital in Indianapolis (now Indiana University Health Methodist Hospital). At the time of the hospital's centennial anniversary in 1999, it had achieved more than a run-of-the-mill hospital. It was the site of the largest neurocritical care unit in the country. It was the hospital where the first heart transplant in a private hospital in the world was conducted, by Dr. Harold Halbrook. It was one of only two Level 1 trauma centers in the area. Today, as Indiana University Health Methodist Hospital, it is the largest health care provider in the state of Indiana.

And it was founded by teenagers.

In July 1899, the Methodist Church's Epworth League, the day's equivalent of youth and young adult ministry (a precursor to United Methodist Youth Fellowship), held a convention in Indianapolis. At the time, Indianapolis had three other hospitals. Yet with persistent diseases that still lacked vaccines, the hospitals were forced to turn away one out of every two patients. Almost all were poor. Inspired by the need, the youth of the Epworth League challenged the Methodist Church to start a hospital. The youth raised $4,750 to prove they weren't kidding. According to the US Department of Labor's Bureau of Labor Statistics, $4,750 in the early 1900s is equivalent to more than $100,000 today, which shows that this wasn't some Saturday morning car wash for a trip to Disneyland.

These kids thought big. The Methodist Church had invested in its youth, and now the youth were returning the favor with a challenge. These were youth who were shaped by a vision of the End, offering an innovative, generative way to address the social needs of poverty and illness together.

Delegates considered the youth's proposal at the 1899 annual meeting of the Indiana Conference of the Methodist Episcopal Church. A report of the meeting indicates that "opposition was not absent." One of the preachers, Dr. B. F. Rollins, said, "Brethren, we have all we can carry on our Church. Now you have come to put upon it one million dollars. Great God, men, where are we going to stop? I am opposed to this hospital proposition."

The meeting's report indicates that a young preacher, the Rev. George M. Smith, who had never before addressed the conference, responded. "Men," he said, "in reply to this brother's question as to where we are going to stop, if I understand our Methodist Episcopal Church, it is not looking for a place to stop. The Church does not dare stop until it encompasses all the interests of Jesus Christ and our Church can never encompass all His interests and leave out sick people."

Reverend Smith's speech, focused on the End, turned the tide. The Conference voted to approve the creation of the hospital, a vote that has had enormous impact on the health and well-being for citizens of Indiana for more than a century.

Christians ought never be looking for a place to stop, much less to go back to Egypt. Who knows what can happen when Christians keep discovering that the End is our beginning?

Almost fifty years earlier, in 1859, a different group of Methodists founded a new college, Valparaiso, in northern Indiana. Who in their right minds would have started a college in 1859, when the economy was in shambles and the United States was on the cusp of a civil war? Immigrant Christians, that's who. People living from the End, aware that their future, and the future of their children and grandchildren, would benefit tremendously from higher education.[11]

This same spirit continues to thrive wherever Christians remain focused on God's reign and the possibilities for social innovation. In contemporary contexts, we discover this spirit more often in the majority world than in established contexts of the United States.

The United Methodist Women of Cote d'Ivoire are organized into small groups to cultivate a variety of microfinance opportunities. Their strategy of making soap as a form of income and for their congregations echoes the more well-known practices of Muhammad Yunus and the Grameen Bank that won Yunus the Nobel Peace Prize in 2006. Yet the Ivorian women have developed their practices less as an example of contemporary interest in microfinance, and more as an extension of the early Wesleyan movement, guided by the power of the Holy Spirit's vision for human flourishing. They have networks of women working together to empower new life in the future.

---

11. Though Valparaiso was founded by Methodists, since the early twentieth century it has been affiliated with the Lutheran Church–Missouri Synod.

43

The Indiana youth in 1899, the immigrant Methodists in 1859, and the Ivorian women in 2008 developed remarkable patterns of social innovation in very different eras and contexts. Yet what they share in common is even more important: an orientation toward God's reign, a belief that God is active in the world, and a willingness to think big.

The Epworth League youth, the immigrant Wesleyans in northern Indiana, and the Ivorian women admirably embodied the five characteristics of social entrepreneurs named in the introductory overview. They shared a passion to serve the mission of God and to bear witness to God's reign by identifying deep social needs and pursuing opportunities to address them. They were marked by small groups of accountability, which were communally attentive to the workings of the Holy Spirit. From these key characteristics stemmed their willingness to adapt, innovate, and learn; act boldly even in uncertain conditions; and hold each other accountable to their collective mission. From out of their Wesleyan tradition sprang their willingness to think big, innovate, and create.

Indeed, at times in American culture, Christians thought big like the youth of the Epworth League or the immigrants in Valparaiso, and we are now their beneficiaries. They founded colleges and universities, hospitals and children's homes, cathedrals and symphonies. Yet, in contemporary America, thinking big seems to have become the provenance of Hollywood, medical research, or technology development.

We have lost the imagination and improvisation, the blessing and the hope that comes with a clear sense of our purpose: our "why." We have become preoccupied with the present: the "what" and the "how." We are too worried about survival, declining numbers, budget cuts, and diminished influence in society to re-discover what it means to think big, shaped by the new beginnings that come with a focus on the End. We reassure ourselves that God calls us to faithfulness, not success, which is half true. But too often we allow other entities to determine what success means and use "faithfulness" as a misguided justification for aiming low and settling for mediocrity. At our worst, we turn faithfulness into nostalgia, and suddenly Egypt becomes the right direction to go.

As Christians today, thinking big just might mean nothing less than recovering the social innovation spirit of our theological forebears in England and the United States (and throughout the world), and our contemporary brothers and sisters in the majority world. That may no longer mean starting hospitals or universities, or maybe it does. There are no doubt other ways to innovate, adapt, and learn as we embrace our mission, act boldly in uncertain times, and hold one another accountable in our mission to bear witness to God's reign. But we have to start thinking differently, again, if we're to see them.

"What causes you to become discouraged?" I asked young Christian leader Katho Bungishabaku, who was visiting Duke Divinity School in the mid-2000s from the eastern part of Congo. I had an hour set aside to visit with him and to learn about what he was doing. I began the conversation by asking him that question, hoping to uncover what he was most worried about.

Bungishabaku had started a university in eastern Congo just a couple of years prior. He talked about the urgent need for education and how the school had grown from 200 to 500 to 800 students in a matter of years and was even beginning to add new areas of study. The school trained pastors, but now also educated people to do work in agriculture and health care. He was hoping to get up to 2,500 students or more.

This was impressive considering the Congolese university is in a region that has been afflicted with some of the worst hatred and violence anywhere in the world. It's an unlikely place to think of starting an institution, much less a university.

The visitor responded to my question this way: "Oh, I never get discouraged." Then he added, "Well, yes, there was one time—when I was confronted by a twelve-year-old with an AK-47. I don't get too worried if I encounter an armed adult, because I can usually talk him out of whatever he's planning to do. But with a twelve-year-old, it's different. They will almost always kill you because they think they have to obey orders. When I was miraculously spared, I realized that I would focus on making use of my time in service to God and never become discouraged."

I had already survived two budget meetings and had grown discouraged at least three times that day. Here was a fellow, a disciple of Christ, who was a lot like Moses in Numbers 12: he was humble in his trust and dependence on God, a humility that led him to be bold and extraordinarily imaginative in creating an institution, a university, in the most unlikely of circumstances. He also knew why he was doing what he is doing.

My friend is probably a lot like those young people were in the Epworth League in 1899, a lot like those immigrant Wesleyans in Valparaiso. Empowered by their intimate friendship with God, and their vision of God's reign, they became a blessing to people around them by embodying hope, cultivating forgiveness and friendship, imagination and improvisation, in the development of institutions of healing as well as education. The odds were against all of them if it was entirely up to them, for they each were in one or another kind of wilderness. Fortunately for them and for us, it wasn't entirely up to them and it still isn't.

Throughout history and around the world, we've found ourselves in the wilderness in a variety of situations, often born out of sin, brokenness, and other kinds of economic and social calamities. In recent years, this has included 9/11, anxieties about global terrorism, and financial crises. Yet times of crisis and anxiety have often been the times when Christians have proved most adventuresome in starting new institutions, in innovating existing institutions, in sustaining new forms of witness to God's reign. Perhaps it's in the wilderness that we discover most clearly who God is and what God is calling us to be and to do.

The End is our beginning, and the source of manifold new beginnings. Only from there can we think big, lead humbly, and innovate on our tradition and reclaim our identity as witnesses to God's inbreaking reign. From our End, we take our cues as actors in the theater of God's glory. We start with the why.

Chapter 2

LOVE MADE ME AN INVENTOR

Practicing Traditioned Innovation

Framing the Perspective

In times of uncertainty, we're inclined to stick to what we know—or think we remember. But rather than heading back to Egypt, we need to develop a mindset called "traditioned innovation." Traditioned innovation honors and engages the past while adapting to the future because it forces us to ask fundamental questions about who we are and what purpose we have for existing: Who have we been, and now, in shifting circumstances, who will we continue to be? How will we stay true to the End, to which God calls us, while adapting to new circumstances? How do we ensure our "why" doesn't change even as we innovate and adapt to changing circumstances?

Christian social innovation depends on a mindset of traditioned innovation in order to hold together the future and the past to shape purposeful, transformative life in the present. To begin exploring what's at stake, I return to the story of Israel in Numbers. Forty years pass and, with it, a generation of Israelites. They have been wandering in the wilderness. Now God calls them to rediscover their End.

The Israelites prepare themselves to enter the promised land. There is a second census and a reorganization of the people. At the Meeting Tent, rules of worship are given again. They are told how they are to enter the land and inhabit it. It's another moment of institution building, or at least a reconstitution of their identity as God's holy people on their way to the promised land. They now know their "why": they're reconstituted as Israel, and they're refocused on their End. They know who they are and where they are going.

Yet in the middle of their preparations, a few of them begin to notice that things have changed. They are reconstituted as Israel, but the circumstances are not quite the same. One of the Israelites, a man named Zelophehad, dies, leaving behind five daughters and no sons. Without a male heir in a patriarchal society, who will receive his inheritance? Who will inhabit the lands on the far bank of the Jordan once promised to him? What will become of his daughters? When they first set out from Egypt, they were given a system by which land was to be distributed. But now there's a new dilemma, which an old system cannot resolve.

The daughters of Zelophehad do something out of the ordinary. They come to Moses and ask him to reevaluate the system by which land is given. "Why should our father's name be taken away from his clan because he didn't have a son?" they ask. "Give us property among our father's brothers" (Num 27:4 CEB). As his daughters, they, too, are called to the land. Yet within the old system, there is no provision for them. Moses consults with the Lord, and the daughters are given the land. They adapt the old system, create innovation, in order to stay true to their calling.

The Israelites' renewed focus on the End oriented their thinking about how to be faithful to the past even as they leaned into new patterns for the future. It helped them discern and clarify what needs to be preserved and what needs to be abandoned for continued faithfulness to God. They recognized the importance of avoiding ceaseless change, on one hand, or stagnant traditionalism, on the other. They embodied a commitment to traditioned innovation.

Traditioned innovation is a way of thinking and living that holds the past and future together in creative tension, a habit of being that depends on wise judgment, requiring both a deep fidelity to the patterns of the past that have borne us to the present and a radical openness to the changes that will carry us forward. Our feet are firmly on the ground with our hands open to the future.

Traditioned innovation is an important mindset to have in any circumstance. It is even more crucial in times of instability, in wilderness circumstances, in contexts where we often feel overwhelmed by all the new things that surround us already—times like the present. Change is happening so fast and furious that it feels disorienting. It feels as though the deep trends I mentioned in chapter 1 are causing the tectonic plates of culture to shift so that we aren't quite sure where it is safe to stand. It is not only that we have lost sight of our End; we find ourselves traversing terrain that is utterly unfamiliar to us.

Our first temptation is to become nostalgic for a past that never was, to imagine that things were better in Egypt than they really were, to pretend that there is a safe place to go where change doesn't happen. We become traditionalists where we want nothing to change around us. At some level, we know we can't live in the past (especially one we don't remember accurately), nor can we create an unchanging present. But too often we engage in unproductive behaviors that run counter to our own best interests, and we become fearful and anxious. Whether we respond externally by furthering social brokenness or internally through depression that furthers personal brokenness, or both, we tend to intensify the problems rather than discover generative solutions.

Our second temptation is to become amnesiacs, and to cultivate change for change's sake. We respond to the disruption around us by focusing on being disruptive forces ourselves. We imagine that anything "new" is "improved" and we cast out anything and everything from the past. In recent years, Clayton Christensen has written provocatively about "disruptive innovation" in business as well as in the social sector.[1] There is significant wisdom in key parts of his argument, to which I will return. Unfortunately, too many people have latched on to the term *disruption* to make it less a description than a normative recommendation—go out and disrupt the status quo in an organization or industry. Unceasing disruption or change is so destabilizing and chaotic that it makes us flip back toward wanting nothing to change.

These wild pendulum swings now characterize much of our life: hoping that nothing will change and then hoping that everything will change, back and forth. This has happened in debates about higher education; some advocate changing *everything*, especially as a result of the emerging digital era, which generates

---

1. See, for example, Clayton M. Christensen, *Disrupting Class* (New York: McGraw-Hill, 2010).

traditionalist responses that *nothing* should change. Within the church we have seen these swings in the "worship wars" and in broader American society in the "culture wars."

We are hungry for innovation, but we need more than change or disruption; we are hungry for innovation that is traditioned, that connects us to the best of our past and to our deepest yearnings and hopes for a life-giving End—for ourselves, for our communities and organizations, and for the world. This is true even for secular contexts most focused on creativity and most oriented toward change. Eric Weiner, in a fascinating book, *The Geography of Genius*, observes that "the past matters. We can't innovate without building on the past, and we can't build on the past unless we know it."[2]

Weiner even notes that it is one of the "myths" of that contemporary hotbed of disruptive innovation, Silicon Valley, that it is "wholly tradition-free, a place that exists in the near future, with no regard for the past." Weiner invokes in support of his view the authority of no less a disruptive innovator than Steve Jobs, who said, "You can't really understand what is going on now unless you understand what came before."[3]

We would recognize the importance of the past for the present if our metaphors were more centrally organic rather than mechanistic. And it is not only single organisms we are called to think about but more determinatively large ecosystems in which organisms move through diverse life-cycles. More than a half-century ago, John Gardner perceptively noted, "For an ever-renewing society the appropriate image is a total garden, a balanced aquarium

---

2. Eric Weiner, *The Geography of Genius* (New York: Simon and Schuster, 2016), 268.

3. Ibid., 310.

or other ecological system." He adds that "the processes of growth, decay and renewal must give due emphasis to both continuity and change in human institutions."[4] Innovation is rooted in the organic requirement of self-renewal, and that requires attention both to the past (continuity) as well as the future (change).

The importance of the past for the present and future ought to be even clearer to Christians, for we are called to witness to the God who is the source of all innovation. Indeed, only God is pure innovation; only God creates out of nothing. In this sense, only God is a true "entrepreneur." Humanity is always "creating" in response to that which has gone before us. Ironically, Weiner recognizes that what people think about "creation" matters significantly, only to misunderstand the Jewish and Christian accounts of origins. Weiner even conflates God and humanity. He writes, "In the Judeo-Christian tradition, it is possible—indeed admirable—to create something ex nihilo, from nothing. This is what God did in creating the world, and that is what we humans aim to do, too."[5]

This is what secular humans aim to do in the West, perhaps, after we have displaced God and yet still aim to act like God. Or, more accurately, in "a secular age" it is what all of us, secular and religious alike, are prone to do. We remain in an "immanent frame" and either unwittingly or wittingly feel like it is up to us to act as if we are God.

Yet faithful Christians and Jews ought to know otherwise. We are not God, nor are we to act as though we are God. Rather, we are called to bear witness to God through traditioned innovation; our activity and creativity are never pure invention or innovation

---

4. Gardner, *Self-Renewal*, 5.
5. Weiner, *Geography of Genius*, 85.

but rather *responsive* to God, the gift of creation, and the given-
ness of reality. We remain dependent creatures; it is a sign of brokenness, and our sin, when we pretend we are autonomous or
self-creating beings. We are always *preceded*.

We are also always *succeeded*. We live toward a future that is
ultimately shaped and determined by God. We are expected to
be creative and innovative in bearing witness to God, but it is
ultimately not up to us. Traditioned innovation enables us to hold
together in creative tension the orientation toward the End with
an appreciation of the best of what has gone before us.

It also involves our casting aside those things that precede
us—individually, communally, organizationally, culturally—that
need to be cast aside because of sin, evil, or simply because they
are no longer relevant. In our personal lives we engage in ongoing
Christian practices to unlearn patterns of sin as we learn patterns
of holy living as expressions of our new life in Christ. But we do
not cast everything off from our prior life; we maintain continuity in our personal identity even as we become new people by the
power of the Spirit.

There is a similar call for communities, organizations, and
cultures. We need to know what to preserve and what to cast off
in order for our innovation to be faithful, effective, and genuinely creative rather than cacophonous and chaotic. Traditioned
innovation involves neither being wedded to the past nor casting it completely off. Jaroslav Pelikan offers an important contrast. "Tradition," he observes, "is the living faith of the dead,
traditionalism is the dead faith of the living."[6] We have too much
experience of traditionalism, which tempts us just to get rid of

---

6. Jaroslav Pelikan, *The Vindication of Tradition* (New Haven, CT: Yale University Press, 1986), 65.

everything and try to start from scratch rather than to carry forward those traditions that are authentically signs of life.

Rediscovering Wesleyan Witness and Scriptural Imagination

The Wesleyan revival of the eighteenth century practiced traditioned innovation in significant ways. John and Charles Wesley immersed themselves in doctrines, practices, and traits of the broad Christian tradition in both its Western and Eastern forms. They exhibited deep fidelity to what had gone before them, even as they sought to breathe new life into Christian witness through innovative experiments.

For example, the small groups (called "class meetings" and "bands") at the heart of the Wesleyan movement were remarkably innovative, yet they drew on diverse patterns of the past such as the early Christian catechumenate and the early modern Pietists. The class meetings and bands were central to the Wesleyan movement's witness to the transformation of individuals, communities, and congregations, even as they also embodied institutional innovation.

The Wesleys cultivated innovative experiments that would help participants in their movement become more deeply engaged with Christian traditions, ranging from the Kingswood School through the Christian Library to various forms of Christian Conference. They also developed innovative institutions such as the Foundry Society, drawing on the traditions of Christian engagement with the poor: the Society developed a lending stock, poorhouses, and a medical dispensary. These demonstrated Wesley's pastoral wisdom and innovation to treat both symptoms and systems of poverty, empowering many Methodists not merely to survive but to live sustainably and even flourish.

The Wesleyan movement in the eighteenth century was shaped by a vision of the outpouring of the Holy Spirit who is making all things new by conforming us to Christ. This emphasis on the Spirit's work—in the lives of people, communities, and institutions—led them both to focus on future possibilities while remaining focused on Christ, in whom all things were originally created.

A primary focus on the Holy Spirit is at the heart of traditioned innovation. The early Church discovered this as the first followers of Christ sought to live into the new reality inaugurated and embodied in Jesus's life, death, and resurrection. The outpouring of the Holy Spirit simultaneously inspired and bewildered these followers. What did the Holy Spirit's presence and work mean for their own lives and communities? What would it mean for Gentiles who became followers of Jesus?

The outpouring of the Holy Spirit at Pentecost was the visible inauguration of the Church as a new community made possible by Jesus Christ. As Luke tells the story, Pentecost provides the hinge between the conclusion of his Gospel and the beginning of the Christian movement as told in Acts. It was a day that was as exciting as it was disorienting, and it set a trajectory for the early Church's ongoing attempt to understand the power of the new in the light of the old. Acts is a story of traditioned innovation.

Pentecost is profoundly new, a radical new beginning, and yet it can only be understood and lived in the light of the Old Testament. As Kavin Rowe notes,

> Luke draws upon a Jewish tradition that associated the feast of Pentecost (Weeks) with the giving of the Jewish Law at Sinai.

Knowing this allows us to see that the event in Jerusalem is narrated as the new Sinai, the new bond of God with his people on the other side of the promises of renewal heralded, for example, in Jeremiah 31 and Ezekiel 11. At Pentecost God gives "a new heart and a new spirit" (Ezekiel 11:19).[7]

The appearance of the Holy Spirit is at once a fulfillment of the promises of Old Testament traditions and a decisive sign of a new beginning of God with God's people. The work of the Holy Spirit who is making all things new is none other than the Spirit who conforms us to Jesus Christ who, as John 1 and Colossians 1 remind us, is the One in whom the very creation came into being.

This beginning of a new age embraces both past and future together: it fulfills the promises of God in the past, and it requires that new patterns of community life be developed and formed. Rowe explains,

> Thus does Luke interpret the coming of the Holy Spirit through the lens of the book of Joel and declare that the "last days" in which God's Spirit will be poured out have now arrived (Acts 2:16-21). And thus does Luke immediately speak of the necessity for devotion "to the apostles' teaching and fellowship, to the breaking of bread and the prayers" and the subsequent new community and its remarkable patterns of life. (Acts 2:42)

The dramatic tension of a present that embraces both future and past, empowered by the Holy Spirit, is thrilling and destabilizing. How do we make sense of it all? How can we discern

---

7. C. Kavin Rowe, "Pentecost as Traditioned Innovation," *Faith & Leadership*, April 27, 2009, https://www.faithandleadership.com/content/pentecost-traditioned-innovation. My description of Pentecost is dependent on Rowe's insightful description in this article. Rowe's broader reflections on Acts in his book *World Upside Down* (New York: Oxford, 2010) are also extremely important for understanding traditioned innovation in early Christianity.

patterns of the old in the light of the new, and patterns of the new in the light of the old?

In Acts, we see the early Christians engaging in ongoing "traditioning," learning what it means to live in the light of God's work in the world: people are baptized, they learn through teaching and fellowship, they receive and offer hospitality in the breaking of bread, and they pray. Rowe observes that

> fulfillment is unintelligible apart from that which is fulfilled (tradition), and life within the new reality requires ongoing organization and education in the patterns that sustain a group whose common purpose is consistently to figure forth the innovation of the Holy Spirit. More simply said, even dramatic innovation will always require tradition.

What happens, though, when the traditions and the new experiences seem to be in conflict? How do the early Christians discern what is of the Holy Spirit from temptations of other spirits? How do we ensure that we are deeply faithful to the traditions that have borne us into the present, while simultaneously bearing witness to the innovation being brought by the outpouring of the Holy Spirit? Can old and new be held together? Is there deep fidelity to the promise of what has already been received?

These questions are ongoing realities in a living tradition. A particular form of the question threatened to fracture the early Christian movement: Do Gentile followers of Jesus Christ need to become Jewish, signified by circumcision, in order to be a part of the Christian community?

Plausible arguments were offered on each side. On one hand, circumcision was a central feature of the Jewish tradition, and Jesus announced that he had come to fulfill the Law and the Prophets (Matt 5:17). The outpouring of the Holy Spirit, on the other hand, seemed to mark a decisive new beginning: the mission to the Gentiles. If tradition and innovation could be put in opposition, the decision would be easier: either stick with the old and risk becoming traditionalists, or make a clean break with everything and do something completely new.

Instead, the Council of Jerusalem entered into a process of discernment. After much discussion, debate, and prayer, they reach the following conclusion that they conveyed in a message to the believers of Gentile origin in Antioch, Syria, and Cilicia:

> The Holy Spirit has led us to the decision that no burden should be placed on you other than these essentials: refuse food offered to idols, blood, the meat from strangled animals, and sexual immorality. You will do well to avoid such things. Farewell. (Acts 15:28-29 CEB)

They conclude that Gentile followers do not need to be circumcised in order to be a member of the Christian movement.

The Council's solution reflects the wisdom of traditioned innovation. Note the words of the conclusion: it is focused on discernment of the Holy Spirit and all of "us." The key to the practice is not what *I* want, or *you* want, in a battle of political power; rather it is rooted in a faithful traditioning process that is simultaneously open to the newness of the Holy Spirit's work in conforming us to Christ.

The wisdom of the Council's judgment only emerges out of the hard work of leaders who were formed deeply in the ways of God and whose imagination is guided by the End of God's reign. Such wisdom is reflected throughout the early Christian movement, from stories in Acts through Paul's letters to the ongoing work of Christians through the centuries. It is wisdom that emerges from an ongoing commitment to Spirit-guided traditioned innovation.

Cultivating a Christian Vision for Today

How do we know today when we are faithfully embodying a commitment to traditioned innovation that is guided by the Holy Spirit?

Spirit-guided traditioned innovation leads us to focus on blessing and hope in nurturing "third way" strategies. The Holy Spirit who is making all things new does so by guiding the world, communities and organizations, and our own lives into transformative, life-giving opportunities. The God who blessed the world and human beings in creation continues to bless in the present, especially by redeeming all that is broken. We are to be what Nicholas Wolterstorff calls "aching visionaries" shaped by Jesus's beatitudes. We are called to see what God is doing in the world, be bearers of blessing, and thus ache with longing for redemption for all who suffer and all who bears marks of sin and brokenness.[8] The blessing we offer as a part of traditioned innovation isn't just about saying nice things or having a positive affirmation for others; it is focused on transformation from brokenness to healing, from fragmentation to wholeness, from sin to holiness.

Similarly, traditioned innovation is Spirit-guided when it is shaped by Christian virtues such as hope. We become focused on the End of God's reign, even as we are attentive to the pain and suffering of the world, of our communities, of others, and of our

---

8. Nicholas Wolterstorff, *Lament for a Son* (Grand Rapids, MI: Eerdmans, 1987), 84–86.

own lives. As Paul notes in Romans 8, we groan with the whole creation for release from our bondage to decay:

> We know that the whole creation is groaning together and suffering labor pains up until now. And it's not only the creation. We ourselves who have the Spirit as the first crop of the harvest also groan inside as we wait to be adopted and for our bodies to be set free. (vv. 22-23 CEB)

Such focus on blessing and hope will help us look for "third way" strategies beyond our fears and anxieties about the future and the impasses where we find ourselves stuck. We embody a commitment to traditioned innovation when we engage strategies and techniques that keep us focused positively on the future through the virtue of hope. These include organizational strategies such as Asset-Based Community Development, which begins by identifying assets in a local community, rather than problems, and seeks to mobilize those assets and build on them in strengthening the community and enhancing its sustainability.[9] Such strategies need to be supplemented by a realistic, at times even pessimistic, awareness of sin and brokenness, but it is crucial that we find techniques to move us away from our tendency toward beginning (and often ending) with fearful, anxious, or even bitter assessments.

Third way strategies, emphasizing blessing and hope, also emerge when we cultivate "opposable" rather than oppositional thinking. Roger Martin defines opposable thinking as "the ability to face constructively the tension of opposing ideas and, instead of choosing one at the expense of the other, generate a creative

---

9. Similar approaches are found in "appreciative inquiry" as an approach to group discussion and facilitation, or in "generative solutions" as an approach to dealing with wicked problems.

resolution of the tension in the form of a new idea that contains elements of the opposing ideas but is superior to each."[10] This is *not* a compromise between the two positions, nor must the new idea contain equal parts of the original ideas. The new idea must transcend the limitations of both original ideas, resolve the tension between them, and do so without violating the internal integrity of each.

Persistent sin and brokenness train us to think in oppositional terms. We define ourselves by what we hate, and we think our ideas will only triumph if others are shown to be faulty. Our educational systems and practices tend to reinforce such oppositional thinking in the assignments we give, such as asking people to write a critique—that is, find what's wrong with another's position.

Oppositional thinking and living causes human life to shrink, to lead us to want to go "back to Egypt." It is one of the chief consequences of sin, and of the sins that too often mark our personal, communal, and institutional lives. By contrast, *opposable thinking* and living cause our worlds to expand and be enriched: Jesus's announcement and embodiment of God's reign, his twofold Great Commandment, and even his call to us to practice forgiveness and reconciliation—including loving our enemies—all reflect an opposable rather than an oppositional pattern. Wesleyan witness at its best has consistently been marked by opposable thinking and living.

Martin's image of opposable thinking is drawn from the analogy of our opposable thumb, which distinguishes us from other animals. As with our opposable thumb, we are capable of holding ideas together that might otherwise been seen as oppositional.

---

10. Roger Martin, *The Opposable Mind* (Cambridge, MA: Harvard Business Review Press, 2007), 15.

And this creativity enables us to find "third ways," constructive alternatives that draw people together into what 1 Timothy calls the "life that really is life" (1 Tim 6:19 NRSV) and generate new patterns of innovative thinking, practices, and institutions.

Spirit-guided traditioned innovation cultivates friendships in which we discover in ever-deeper and ever-richer ways the power of God's forgiveness for the sake of a vibrant future. We are created for friendship—with God, with each other, and even with ourselves. Yet in a world marked by sin and brokenness, we not only think in oppositional ways, we also often define ourselves by our enemies and those from whom we are estranged. Often, like Jonah, we shrink and shrivel when we encounter God's gracious love for our enemies—sometimes angrily and defiantly telling God over and over again we would rather die than see others forgiven. Jonah reminds us that it isn't enough to *know* that God is a God of love, forgiveness, and hope; we can know that and still be resentful (see Jonah 4:1-11).

Rather, we need to learn—in our thinking and feeling and perceiving and living—the fullness of life that really is life. And we need friends along the way to help us in that learning. We need the perspective that friends offer. Sin at its heart involves self-deception; we don't have accurate readings of who we really are and what we really do. Sometimes we think too highly of ourselves, sometimes we think too lowly of ourselves, and often we are just confused or deceived about ourselves. And there are different temperaments, experiences, and social contexts that intensify the challenges we face in self-understanding. Other people, when they have our best interests at heart, offer light on our lives, the world, and the challenges and opportunities that we face. They are not only friends with whom we share important things in common; they are holy friends who join with us in discernment, guided by the Holy Spirit, into a transformational, life-giving future.

Holy friends pull us out of ourselves, calling forth the best from us by helping us see as God sees. Rather than shrinking from fear, anxiety, anger, or bitterness, we discover the blessing and hope that leads us into a more innovative, life-giving future. In the process, we also learn how to draw on the past in redemptive ways. By orienting us toward blessing and hope, friends enable us to learn forgiveness as a way of life. And in learning forgiveness as a way of life, we learn to cast aside both amnesia and traditionalist nostalgia for the sake of a commitment to traditioned innovation.

This link between forgiveness and friendship in traditioned innovation offers a distinctive lens on discussions of innovation and entrepreneurship. We too often mistakenly think of innovation as something isolated individuals do. We imagine genius teenagers like Bill Gates, Steve Jobs, or Mark Zuckerberg in their garages or dorm rooms, inventing new gadgets or approaches. This wasn't true of those people, and it is even less true of innovation and entrepreneurship more generally. Careful research into successful innovation and entrepreneurship shows they are "team sports"; we flourish in teams, communities, and even more so through embodied friendship where people engage and inspire each other. That typically includes people who offer diverse gifts to each other, something Christians should already have realized as a part of our DNA given Paul's reminder in 1 Corinthians 12.

Spirit-guided traditioned innovation is nurtured by imagination and improvisation; these lead to scalable experiments that, when successful, create a new equilibrium. The Holy Spirit guides us into spaces where we can accomplish "abundantly far more" than all we can ask or imagine on our own (Eph 3:20-21 NRSV). Holy friends help us cultivate that imagination as we build on the past and learn from it.

The Holy Spirit also guides us to become improvisational in our approaches. We live in act four of God's five-act drama, and since God is responsible for the final act (i.e., the kingdom in its fullness) we have the freedom to experiment. Such experimentation, though, depends on us nurturing mindsets and skills that are rooted in improvisation, rather than just trying to make things up as we go along. Improvisation is a great jazz ensemble; making things up is a bad version of a middle-school band concert. What mindsets and skills do we need to develop to nurture improvisation?

First, we adopt *learning as a way of life*. This is part of a traditioning process, of holding together the future and the past. Jazz musicians are always learning: how to become better at playing their own instruments, how to master core repertoires that enables them to connect to other musicians, how to be attentive and listen to others around them. So also for us as Christians: we need to be engaged in lifelong learning of the scriptures and Christian traditions, enabling us to become more and more fluent in the wisdom that is a gift to us from God. This entails the cultivation of habits of thinking, feeling, perceiving, and living through Christian practices that nurture a "scriptural imagination."

Further, Christians need to be attentive to learning from diverse fields and disciplines, stirring our imagination and helping us see connections that we might not otherwise see. And we need to be listening to others' perspectives on our own lives, our communities and organizations, so that we can be engaged in the ongoing process of unlearning sin and learning holiness and wisdom.

If we develop a learning mindset, we can bring things together into a meaningful story: past, present, and future are held together in a vision that enables us to grow. We don't get lost in the past, or absorbed in fantasies about the future, or stuck in a paralyzed present. Further, a learning mindset enables us to grow from failures. The slogan of the innovative design firm IDEO is "fail quickly so you can succeed sooner." But that only works if we know how to learn from those failures, whether culpable or experimental, and change and grow as a result.

A learning mindset also helps us think and live opposably rather than oppositionally. We become imaginative in looking for third ways, rather than getting stuck in thinking that what currently exists is all that could possibly be. We become improvisational.

Second, we *live into traditioned innovation by saying "yes" or "yes, and" as our default way of engaging others.* Whenever possible we live into the future with a spirit of saying "yes" to all that is in front of us. And if we can't say a simple "yes," we are then encouraged to say "yes, and" so that we can find creative paths forward. Improvisers call this "overaccepting."

Oppositional thinking means we tend to "block" what others offer, finding what's wrong or rejecting their perspective. In *Improvisation*, Sam Wells proposes that Christians should aim to avoid blocking. Accepting with a "yes" assumes a context of trust, in which the attainment of one person's good is intimately linked to the good of others (especially friends). It assumes that we live in an environment of abundant resources, enlivened by the Holy Spirit who is making all things new, where the goods that truly matter are inexhaustible, and where individuals don't seek *their own share* but instead seek *to share.* Those who accept and overaccept don't seek to control or manipulate the future; rather, they open themselves to God's unexpected surprises. At our best, those who accept learn how to say "yes" to others and to God, which might be a succinct description of heaven.

Yet we live in a fallen world, where saying "yes" to certain offers can range from naïveté to foolishness to outright cooperation with evil—especially in the case of authoritarian political movements, systemic injustice, and sexual or financial misconduct. A natural and understandable impulse is simply to block these offers, and the church has at times found "no" to be the only faithful response to various sinful offers. But every "no" comes with costs: shrinking the imagination, shutting down avenues toward redemption, or relinquishing the capacity to interpret the world in God's most charitable light. In these kinds of situations, both "accepting" and "blocking" produce problematic results, which leave us in that state of frustrated isolation we need to move beyond.

"Yes, and" is not about compromise; we are not trying to find some common ground *between* "accepting" and "blocking." We improvise most effectively when we find fruitful ways beyond the impasse because we are not morally obligated to say "no." The first impulse of the overaccepting improviser is not to ask, "What *should* I do here?" or "What *must* I do here?" Instead, she asks, "How *could* I receive this as a gift? What *could* this gift be?" What could happen if I greeted this stranger as Christ, and received their offer as a gift from God? What could this relationship be if I forgive instead of seeking revenge? What could the Church be if overaccepting became a communal instinct, practiced in the midst of friend and enemy alike, always attentive and open to

God's next surprise? How could a new experiment in social innovation bear witness to the truth, beauty, and goodness of God's reign?

We would, third, *become more creative by cultivating connections*. This ought to be a place where Wesleyans, who have emphasized "connection," would find a sweet spot with a trend in our world toward horizontal networks and connections. Those of us who are heirs of John and Charles Wesley and "the people called Methodist" ought naturally to be seeking collaboration, patterns of integrative thinking, and unconventional friendships. Yet United Methodists have too often treated "connection" now as a vertical, bureaucratic strategy for handling finances (i.e., paying money to the denomination) rather than horizontal patterns of creativity and renewal (i.e., connections among fellow Christians in other congregations locally, regionally, and globally).

Improvisation, whether in music or the theater, depends on the ability to learn from those who have gone before us as well as those who are around us. If, and insofar as, we cultivate connections—with diverse ideas, diverse people, diverse sectors—we will likely discover the creativity that enables us to forge life-giving and transformational paths into the future.

As important as it is to cultivate connections, we also need time to preserve our solitude. It is important to learn to listen to God in quiet moments and to reflect deeply on our own individual identity and purpose. Dietrich Bonhoeffer's *Life Together* stresses "the day together" and "the day alone" as complementary ways to live each day. Musically, when you know your own voice (or instrument), you can harmonize better with other voices (or instruments). That harmonization can reauthenticate your own voice, and it depends on both collaboration and solitude.[11]

Mindsets and practices that nurture our imagination and cultivate improvisational skills are crucial, especially in this era where deep trends are causing the tectonic plates of culture to shift so dramatically. Leaning into an imaginative vision for the future is crucial to address disruptive forces affecting institutions (including, but not limited to, the Church), communities, and our own lives. When we are focused on the present and on maintaining the status quo, we tend to be content with incremental change rather than transformation. But the power of God's Holy Spirit calls us to envision and live into a transformational future.

What does this era of disruption and shifting tectonic plates of culture mean for the Church and renewing Wesleyan witness? If we are to live faithfully and effectively into the future in a spirit of Christian social innovation empowered by the Holy Spirit, we need to be willing to take risks. This includes attending to the destabilizing forces in the wider culture, as well as asking questions about why we are not reaching the "unchurched" and "dechurched" around us. This requires imagination and "fresh eyes" to see new possibilities, rather than being content with what we already know and are used to doing.

Our imagination needs to be stretched in new ways. We know the importance of looking to the long-term, embodied in such wisdom as "Feed a person a fish, they eat for a day; teach a person to fish, and they eat for a lifetime." We need to be stretched, though, to realize that sometimes we need to be innovative in seeing the need "to change the nature of the fishing industry." If

---

11. I am grateful to Nathan J. Jones for helping me see the importance of this complementarity.

there are problems with the ecology of the lakes and rivers, or if there aren't any fish there, then teaching alone won't do it. We need a mindset of traditioned innovation to help us look with fresh eyes at the whole fishing industry and see what needs to be changed.

We can be helped to see with fresh eyes by Clayton Christensen's approach to disruptive innovation.[12] Christensen's key insight is that disruptive innovation typically begins when "outsiders" to an established perspective find creative experiments that address needs that are currently not being met or reach new constituencies. Initially there is no competition with the established organization because the disruptive innovation aims at unmet needs and reaching new people.

One of Christensen's key examples is Apple's initial development of personal computers; Apple did not compete with the major mainframe computer companies like DEC and IBM but rather designed personal computers on which kids could play games. Over time Apple became the normative company as its innovations caught hold and became attractive to established constituencies. That is when the threat emerged, but it was a threat only to "old ways" of doing things. It actually offered promise of new approaches that met important needs and reached more people.

Disruptive innovation has been happening in the Church, especially in mainline Protestantism, though we haven't paid sufficient attention to it. For example, parachurch youth and young adult ministries that emerged in the latter half of the twentieth

---

12. Bishop Kenneth H. Carter Jr., Susan Pendleton Jones, and I wrote a series of five articles that engage Christensen's approach as a resource for renewing mainline protestant Christianity in *Faith & Leadership* in late 2013 and 2014.

century—Young Life, Campus Crusade for Christ, Navigators, and InterVarsity—addressed deep trends and met needs that "established" church youth groups and campus ministries had not been able to touch.

In recent decades, these parachurch groups have become the dominant forms of Christian ministry to youth and young adults in the United States, and mainline Protestants (such as United Methodists) have struggled to adapt. We have lacked the imagination to see new ways of engaging young people, and we now struggle with an aging membership. This doesn't bode well for us demographically; neither is it promising for holding together the wisdom of elders with the imagination and the passionate characteristic of young people.

Ironically, we have failed to reach young people in established churches at precisely the same time that young people have been expressing more and more interest in social innovation. The most innovative organizations and cultures tend to "overinvest" in young people like those young people in the Epworth League in Indiana at the dawn of the twentieth century.

Dreaming for Transformation

Clay Christensen notes that it is difficult for established organizations to practice disruptive innovation. It requires experiments, "skunkworks," where a small group of people is assigned to work on innovative ideas that are protected from standard organizational practices. Such skunkworks involve blessing and protection by the leadership of the organization and credibility among those involved in the experiment as well as enough freedom and patience to explore whether the innovations might take hold.

The Wesleyan movement in the eighteenth century was itself a kind of skunkworks in an era of disruption; can we recover the creative mindset of traditioned innovation for our era? Bishop Ken Carter and the Florida Annual Conference of the United Methodist Church are developing a skunkworks through their approach to "fresh expressions" of the gospel.[13] The "Fresh Expressions" movement originated in the early 2000s in the Church of England, and its name is taken from the Book of Common Prayer: "The Church of England...professes the faith uniquely revealed in the Holy Scriptures and set forth in the catholic creeds, which faith the Church is called upon to proclaim afresh in each generation."

Fresh Expressions is a strategy rooted in traditioned innovation. Bishop Carter takes his understanding from the Church of England's definition: "A fresh expression is a form of church for our changing culture, established primarily for the benefit of people who are not yet members of any church. It will come into being through principles of listening, service, contextual mission, and making disciples. It will have the potential to become a mature expression of church shaped by the Gospel and the enduring marks of the church and for its cultural context."

The fresh expressions that Florida Conference churches are developing are faithful to the Christian tradition, developing opportunities to reach people currently not being served, and offer opportunities to invest deeply, even "overinvest," in young people. These fresh expressions are meeting in unconventional places such as boat marinas, running trails, and even bars, and are targeting

---

13. Bishop Carter offered in the fall of 2015 a series of eleven blog reflections on the Fresh Expressions initiative that can be found on the conference's website: http://www.flumc.org/blogs?topic=19984.

constituencies that are underserved (including an experiment to reach a community of registered sex offenders). Some younger clergy and laity are thinking and dreaming big about what can happen as a result of this experiment in Christian social innovation.

As they dream, they, and we, can be inspired and encouraged by the story of a saintly woman named Maggy Barankitse, known to some of the locals in Burundi (a country in central Africa) as the "madwoman from Ruyigi." Maggy seems to be a "madwoman" because she is an exemplary practitioner of Christian social innovation and she has been doing so in one of the poorest countries of the world and in the wake of some of the most horrifying violence imaginable. Maggy embodies traditioned innovation and lives at the intersections of blessing, hope, friendship, forgiveness, imagination, and improvisation.

Who is this woman, what is her vision, and how does she accomplish it? Maggy is a Roman Catholic laywoman in Burundi, ethnically a Tutsi, who as a young adult was a teacher and then a secretary to the Roman Catholic bishop. When a civil war broke out in the early 1990s, the militia came to Ruyigi and committed a massacre in 1993. Maggy was tied to a chair and forced to watch while the militia killed seventy-two people in her community—including priests and nuns and Maggy's best friend, Juliette.

Miraculously, Maggy was allowed to live. After the militia left, she found seven children hiding in the sacristy, children her mother had adopted. She was able to save twenty-five other children as well, including Juliette's children whom Maggy had promised to care for. The larger landscape of the killing field remained, haunting Maggy with memories of death and destruction.

After enduring such atrocities, we might expect an instinct of mere survival, of self-preservation, or even revenge to take over. Maggy, after all, was a woman of some means and connection. Since she had lived and studied abroad, it seems perfectly legitimate to expect that she would find a suitable place for the children, then escape the country as a refugee. Survival, under the circumstances dominating Burundi, seems the most sensible recourse. Who would expect anything different?

But Maggy did the opposite. She remained in Burundi, with her mother's adopted children *and* the twenty-five orphans. In the weeks that followed, she welcomed more and more orphaned and abandoned children into her care. It is said that Maggy never turned a child away. Why would she stay? What rooted her there? Why keep accepting more and more children to care for, when the burdens of doing so would begin to feel overwhelming?

Some years after the October 1993 massacres, a French journalist asked Maggy a similar question, wanting to know what she was thinking in the days following the brutal killings in Ruyigi. Maggy told him,

> As soon as I knew that my children had been saved, I felt a strong will to live! I could think of one thing only: taking care of them. Raising them beyond this hatred...I was there to accompany the young ones and help them find, in themselves, the joy of life, despite the terror of what they'd seen.[14]

She didn't want her own adopted children, or the others in her care, merely to survive the war or escape it as if it never happened. Rather than fleeing the storms of violence and destruction, she walked toward the storm with her children. She believed that

---

14. This story was learned by the author in conversation with Maggy.

the hope of new life is found through pain and suffering—not by fleeing it. She recognized that Christ's resurrection transfigured his wounds; it did not erase them.

Maggy wanted something more, something that neither forgot the past, nor dwelled in it. She wanted to break the "collective amnesia" that continually caused her country to erupt in violence; she also wanted to overcome the bleak hopelessness that can be found if one cannot escape the hauntings of the past. Maggy wanted to bear witness to the Easter that is found on the far side of Good Friday. She wanted to bear witness to God's love, to embody the hope that points toward the fullness of God's reign. She wanted to live in the power of the Holy Spirit who is making all things new.

So she built a swimming pool that sits on the site of the massacre. She wanted the children to swim and have their vision cleansed, she said, as with the waters of baptism. Then she built a movie theater. She wanted the children to laugh and enjoy life. As you look around Ruyigi, it isn't just a swimming pool and movie theater that draw your attention; you see a hospital, a beauty shop, a mechanic shop, Catholic and Protestant churches, an international school, a library, a tailor; the sustainable farm that produces crops, makes cheese, and has a granary; the morgue; the many houses that have sheltered thousands of orphans and families broken by war. None of it should be there.

What she envisioned, and her community has built, is called Maison Shalom, "the House of Peace." It is a whole new world for Ruyigi, a new beginning shaped by a vision of the End of God's reign and by traditions of Christian wisdom. It is a place where for more than two decades thousands of children have been educated, healed, and nurtured. They have learned marketable skills, and they have learned the habits of a faith-filled way of life.

If you ask Maggy how she came to cast this vision for Maison Shalom, a place where orphans of Burundi can be raised beyond the ethnic hatred and cycles of vengeance that plagued the country, she will tell you this: **"Love made me an inventor."** That simple phrase gets to the heart of traditioned innovation: "love" signifies for Maggy the whole story of the Bible, from Genesis to Revelation, of God's creative and redemptive love that will emerge triumphant in the fullness of the kingdom. "Invent" signifies for Maggy the Christian imagination that has led her to cultivate a whole ecosystem of institutions that have changed the equilibrium for children in Burundi, and now in Rwanda and eastern Congo as well.

Maggy's vision for Maison Shalom began to form in the wake of the massacre. She wanted to invent, as she puts it, "a way of living without hate." She longed for her children, and all children, to be able to flourish in a life rooted in blessing and hope. Maggy's vision was rooted in a Christian imagination formed through her lifelong habits and convictions, an imagination that could see together the importance of practices like forgiveness and friendship on the one hand, and the significance of institutions that give shape and form to a way of life on the other.

The practice of forgiveness has been at the heart of Maggy's life and vision; it is also a stony road to tread. It's a mistake to paint too rosy a picture here, to suggest that Maggy moved from the horrors of that October 1993 straight to a vision centered in forgiveness, like some clichéd Hollywood plot that jumps from unavoidable conflict to perfect resolution. Forgiveness didn't come easily for Maggy herself; it was, and still is, a journey. For some time, she wouldn't attend church because she could not bear to participate in communion with those who had murdered her friends.

She cultivated friendships with old allies and new acquaintances, even as she also prayed for and nurtured her own practice of forgiveness and encouraged practices of forgiveness. She started by nurturing relationships between the children of victims and assailants. Justine, an orphan under Maggy's care, had to walk for three years past the house of the people who killed her parents. They never said a word to each other, but Justine attended school with their children. Slowly, over the course of years, the children became friends, a slight crack where forgiveness might find its way into their lives. When it was time to rebuild Justine's home, Maggy convinced those responsible for its destruction to help rebuild it. The man who killed Justine's parents came as well. Seven years after the killing, he finally asked for forgiveness; yes, in actual words, and also through the rebuilding of the home. Forgiveness took the physical form of a man drawing water into a bucket to make bricks to build the home he once destroyed.

For Maggy, building homes was a way both to embody forgiveness and to rebuild a community ravaged by war. She found a way to innovate on her faith's tradition of forgiveness, while discovering that through forgiveness she could rebuild Ruyigi and help restore the lives of its people. Maggy took a fundamental Christian practice and *improvised* on it. Forgiveness became something not only spoken; it was also built out of clay and water, wood and brick.

One day, as Maggy was lamenting the ongoing polarization and violence that emerges out of the collective amnesia of the country and the "blame games" that result, she noted, "We need to get away from blame and begin to build—trust, roads, love, forgiveness."[15] For Maggy, trust, love, and forgiveness belong in the same sentence as roads.

Maggy makes connections. Her synthetic imagination, her ability to see how life flourishes when people are brought together, when words like *trust* and *love* and *forgiveness* are connected to roads and homes and jobs and institutions and leadership—that is where we discover the power of innovation for new life. Maggy was shifting people's mindsets from fear to hope, from a world marked by fragmentation to one that builds bridges—literally and figuratively.

Maggy is frustrated by a tendency of Christians just to focus on social service and social advocacy; she is a social innovator. Maggy asks Western Christians, "Why do you only give us clothes and such? We can dream like you!" Maggy imagines the possibility of transformative change.

All that Maison Shalom has become has emerged out of a Christian view of humanity, of creation and redemption and consummation. Her Christian vision anchors everything. It provides her and the people she serves a sense of their own human dignity because they are God's beloved; it also illumines for her the ways that sin works beyond individual people, infecting entire communities, institutions, and societies.

For Maggy, the overarching story of God's love is never an abstraction; it is a shaping story that is profoundly real and that takes on flesh in the work of Maison Shalom. Why else would Maggy have had the audacity to build a movie theater in the middle of a war? It isn't because she thought the children needed distraction

---

15. Judith Debetencourt Hopkins, *Hummingbird, Why Am I Here? Maggy's Children* (CreateSpace, 2012), 116.

from their circumstances. When the children watch a film, they enter another's story and dream along with them. They see and imagine a different kind of life—a life beyond war, death, poverty, and AIDS. They dream dreams beyond hatred and revenge.

Even the soldiers wanted to dream dreams beyond war. At times the militia, who still had camps down the road, asked to watch movies. Maggy welcomed them, but she insisted they put down their guns before entering the theater. A sign outside the theater, resembling an AK-47 marked over by a circle and red slash, stands guard while the lambs and lions of Burundi sit together in the dark and dream in front of the big screen.

Maggy's learning has been enhanced by her engagement with her children. She notes quickly that Maison Shalom did not emerge only out of her imagination; she has discovered important ideas, remarkably innovative possibilities, from the hope expressed by the children with whom she is working. Maggy's genius is that she combines a deep theological wisdom, a synthetic imagination, and a willingness to listen to the hopes and dreams of young people. Innovation is a team sport.

"Every day I improvise new life," Maggy says. Maggy doesn't believe in the Western preoccupation with strategic planning, because she believes that betrays a lack of confidence in God. "My plan," she says, "is only five letters in the French alphabet: A-M-O-U-R; in English, it is only four: L-O-V-E."[16]

It seems too simple. Yet it has proven astoundingly effective in its impact as well as the visibility of its witness. After all, no strategic planning process would likely have resulted in a decision to build Maison Shalom in the midst of a war, nor would prudent

16. Cited in Emmanuel Katongole, *The Sacrifice of Africa* (Grand Rapids, MI: Eerdmans, 2011), 178.

budgeting have led to the incredible scale and scope of the work and the children whose lives have been transformed.

Love and forgiveness have enabled Maggy to become an inventor and to improvise new life. What we might not notice as clearly is that her innovation has also helped her, the children, and the people of Burundi discover new dimensions of love and forgiveness. Precisely by focusing on a future that is not bound by the destructiveness of the past, by being drawn into creative work that offers new life, people also discover themselves being healed, renewed, and empowered to offer signs of love and forgiveness they otherwise could not have imagined. Love and forgiveness make a future possible; living into an innovative future also makes further love and forgiveness possible for others, and healing and hope for all. It is a virtuous cycle.

But Maison Shalom didn't appear in a day's time, and you don't acquire nicknames like "the madwoman of Ruyigi" without possessing tremendous resilience and grit. Maggy gained her reputation by helping build a road to Maison Shalom in the middle of a battle zone. There are stories of her hiding in the trunks of cars traveling to and from Bujumbura. There were the early years when Maggy would find bodies slung across the fence in front of Maison Shalom, left by assailants to mock the work she was trying to do. Or there were the times Maggy was accused of being a traitor to her Tutsi clan for embracing Hutus. Or the bureaucratic obstacles she had to overcome from local and national government officials. Or the patriarchal attitudes that told her in explicit and subtle ways that women are not supposed to lead but rather should stay home so the men can run things. It would have been easy to lapse back into old mindsets, to become trapped in old patterns of fear, hatred, bitterness, and brokenness.

Maggy's faith and her belief in the new possibilities for life have allowed her to persevere in the face of conditions that would have doomed less resilient and hope-filled people to failure. It took seven years, after all, for Justine and the man who killed her parents to forgive and reconcile with each other. There is no future without forgiveness, and there are no shortcuts to the future; forgiveness requires perseverance and patience and hope, traits born out of Maggy's vision and practices, her willingness to lift her eyes up to God from out of the daily challenges, "to hug everything," as one journalist has said, "even the horizon."

Maggy continues to struggle with the horrors of the past and the challenges of the present. She notes that there are many times when God has felt distant, when she has cried out. Yet she prays every day, listening to God and listening for God. Such is the character of intimacy with God; indeed, those who are closest to God often experience the darkest nights of the soul. After all, their closeness to God makes the realization of the brokenness in the world all that more intense, including one's own limitations and brokenness. They learn to watch the world with Christ in Gethsemane.

Yet in their intimacy with God they also find, like Maggy, the most resilient hope. Maggy says,

> There are always miracles in the Shalom House [i.e., Maison Shalom] because I believe in love. I believe that nobody can stop me. I compare the Shalom House to a train that God conducts. Nobody can stop this train. He will still move it— because God is God. There will be some cars that will stop. But He will continue to gather Congolese, Rwandese, Europeans saying, "Come my children and build my dream."[17]

17. Cited in ibid., 180.

Optimists tend to become embittered because they discover the intractability of problems and the brokenness of fallible human beings. Maggy is resilient not because of her confidence in human beings but because of her trust in God and her hope for the promise of God's future. So (as quoted in the Introductory Overview) she prays every day that the Lord's miracles would break forth and that she would not be an obstacle in any way.

Maggy sensed from the beginning that to help children thrive, the communities in which they live must thrive as well. Maison Shalom now employs more than six hundred people, many of whom are alumni whom she helped raise, alumni who as children helped to shape Maggy's imagination and to dream extraordinary dreams of what might be possible. Maggy rarely asks people directly for help; rather, she casts the vision, telling you stories of what they are trying to do and why—and then trusts that you will want to participate as a result. Her vision, like the Holy Spirit's work, is contagious.

How can we catch visions like Maggy, and be formed in mindsets, practices, and virtues that will shape a commitment to Christian social innovation? We turn in the next chapter to a description of such formation.

Chapter 3

CULTIVATING PRACTICAL WISDOM

Forming Christians for Innovation

Framing the Perspective

Are innovators born or made? Or both? We hear stories about people like Maggy and we marvel with admiration. Yet too often we also secretly say to ourselves, "People like that are just different.... We could never be like Maggy or do what she does." Or could we?

Christians above all should recognize and honor the diversity of gifts among us (1 Corinthians 12). We can honor that people like Maggy are gifted with imagination, charisma, and vision that is exceptional and distinctive. But if innovation is a "team sport," then all of us can participate in innovation in different ways. And to do so, we all need to be formed in mindsets, activities, and traits that support a Christian vision for social innovation. Even those with the most extraordinary gifts, such as Maggy, need friendships and patterns of formation that cultivate those gifts.

This is especially the case when people are anxious and fearful because of uncertain times, or discouraged and bitter because of conditions of systemic suffering and injustice. As a young boy growing up in apartheid South Africa in the 1960s and 1970s, Teboho "Tsietsi" Mashinini blended right in with the crowd as an anonymous "nobody."[1] The apartheid government wanted it that way, too, because masses of anonymous humanity proved much easier to control than named individuals in tight-knit communities. As soon as a young, black boy began living into a name and a story, apartheid began to lose its grip. Once he had gained an identity, he also gained something even more threatening to apartheid: hope.

But those in hopeless situations typically don't invent hopeful solutions on their own. Hope tends to pop up as a relational surprise, an unearned gift from another who knows you and loves you and cares for your future. Mashinini received encouragement from family and teachers who saw potential in him. Of all the relational influences that contributed to Mashinini's newfound hope, however, none left quite as strong a mark as a discipleship group in his local Methodist parish.

There, members of the group challenged assumptions that apartheid had instilled in him: that his life had no value, that he would never amount to anything, and that black South Africans had nothing to hope for. Tsietsi's father had been a lay preacher in the church, so these people knew Tsietsi well. They told him that he had leadership potential, and they encouraged him to see

---

1. I am grateful to the Reverend Peter Storey, who first shared Mashinini's story with me.

his own life story within the context of a larger story of God's kingdom. These strands eventually came together, and he—no, they—began to dream dreams beyond apartheid.

One of those dreams took shape in the mid-1970s, shortly after the apartheid government had announced that the white, colonial language of Afrikaans would become a mandatory language for education. Black students like Mashinini became outraged, feeling an acute blow to their dignity as nonwhite South Africans. In response, Mashinini convened a meeting of nearby student leaders. Together they formed an action committee, which agreed to organize a mass demonstration for students that would take place three days later, on June 16, 1976.

That morning, Mashinini led hundreds of students from his own high school to meet with thousands of others who had gathered from nearby schools. As with many other peaceful demonstrations in nonpeaceful times, the situation quickly turned violent. Police had barricaded their intended marching route, so the students marched along a different one. Eventually, however, police and students collided. Sparked by an incident involving rock-throwing, police began shooting recklessly into the crowd, leaving several hundred bodies in their wake.

Dubbed the "Soweto Uprising," the events of June 16, 1976, mark something of a watershed moment in apartheid resistance. The United Nations Security Council shed international light on the apartheid regime, strongly condemning it with the passage of Resolution 392. Internally, many white South Africans grew troubled at the realization that their government was capable of such violence. Perhaps most importantly, however, the Soweto Uprising gave young, black South Africans hope for a life beyond apartheid—a life that Mashinini now believed was possible.

Chapter 3

Rediscovering Wesleyan Witness and Scriptural Imagination

When young Mashinini believed he was nothing, God used "holy friends" to help him become something. Those holy friends were found centrally in a Methodist discipleship group in Johannesburg, a group that continues a Wesleyan emphasis on forming Christians through weekly meetings—meetings that were a primary focus for the Wesleyan revival of the eighteenth century. Holy friendship is a contemporary formulation of a practice that has shaped and enlivened Wesleyan witness from its origins to the present.

Holy friends address the gap between *who we are*, whether we are seekers or well along our Christian journey, and *who God calls us to be*. Holy friends orient us toward the future of God's reign, keeping us focused on the End, even while they engage us in deep reflection to help us unlearn patterns of sin and learn patterns of holiness. Holy friends help hold together both dimensions of Maggy's prayer: they keep us focused on the Lord's miracles, even as they also help us see ways in which we—often beyond our awareness—are creating obstacles for God's work in the world and in our own lives.

Holy friends hold several things together with and for us: **they challenge sins we have come to love, help us affirm gifts we are afraid to claim, and enable us to dream dreams we otherwise wouldn't have dreamed.** Holy friends do this relationally, so there is no sequence from challenge through affirmation to dreaming. The practices exist in complex interrelation, and often it is through the affirmation and the dreams that we discover fresh ways to receive the challenge of casting off our sins. The Wesleys

88

combined an optimistic, transformational orientation to the future with an acute recognition of our capacity for sin and evil apart from God. They were people of hope.

Holy friends help us to see the world first and foremost through God's eyes, so we can locate ourselves in the larger story of God. We need help from our holy friends, and we in turn offer such hope to them, in order to see God at work in our lives and in the world. Too often our own self-understanding is distorted by sin, by self-deception, by our participation in destructive mind-sets, habits, and practices. Holy friendships reorient us and stir our imaginations. How do they do that?

Sin, and specific sins, hold us back from embracing God's call to live into a better, holier future. This includes things we did or failed to do, as well as things that others have done to us or have failed to do for us. It also includes those broader systemic and historical dynamics that make it difficult for us to see ourselves, our communities and institutions, or even God very clearly.

Holy friends help us discover our patterns of self-deception, and enable us to unlearn sin and to discover forgiveness for our own sins. This is especially important for those sins we have come to love that have become so much a part of us that we find ways to redescribe them to sound like they aren't really problematic. So a person describes their workaholism as "doing the Lord's work," rather than recognizing that keeping the Sabbath and having rhythms of work, rest, and play are integral to faithfulness (and creativity!).

Holy friends do more than challenge our sins, though. If that is all they did, we might need them around, but it wouldn't be very encouraging. They also affirm gifts we are afraid to claim. Often what holds us back from embracing God's call and discovering new life is less our sin and more a fear of the unknown, an inability to see our own gifts, or, as in Mashinini's case, a perceived lack of self-worth caused by others' sin. Holy friends, in these cases, widen our horizons by pointing to a bolder—and holier—future both for us and for others. They affirm gifts we are afraid to claim and help us dream dreams far larger than we otherwise could have imagined.

Those dreams might be both life-changing and, sometimes, world-changing. Who would have ever thought that Mashinini might become a leader in a march in Soweto whose significance was such that its date, June 16, is now a national holiday for South Africa akin to America's July 4? Just as holy friends challenge our sins and affirm our gifts, they also help us imagine new possibilities for ourselves and others. Mashinini could have settled for social activism, but his vision and the engagements he and his friends developed led to a new equilibrium through social innovation.

Social innovation and new institutions regularly emerge out of the exceptional dreams of people. Almost always undergirding and surrounding those people are teams of friends who help to incubate those ideas. We are enabled by holy friends to accomplish, by the power of God at work within us, "far beyond all" we could have asked or imagined otherwise (Eph 3:20-21).

As Mashinini's story illumines, God uses our holy friends to help us grow into people we never could have become on our own. God uses our friends, in other words, to help us cultivate character traits—like Mashinini's courage to lead—we may never even have thought we could develop. Young Mashinini probably never thought he would be described as a "courageous leader" or "social innovator." Yet that's exactly what he had become, owing in large part to the impact that the holy friends from his local Methodist church in Johannesburg had on his life.

To be sure, all this talk of character growth and "becoming somebody" risks placing an undue accent on human effort. The Christian life could devolve into some form of optimism or works-righteousness in which having the "right attitude" or acquiring "enough character" becomes the main focus. Here potential dangers abound, ranging from the despair of one who struggles to grow, to the sinful pride of one who showcases his character traits like sports trophies. Nevertheless, Christian character need not fall victim to these eat-or-be-eaten conceptions of character achievement.

Rather, Christian character develops as an achievement we receive as a gift. That is, our character is formed over time through friendships and practices that are themselves faithful, *free* responses to the inbreaking of God's grace. Notice, for example, that the upward trajectory of Mashinini's story doesn't begin with his own personal desire to "become somebody." It begins instead as a surprise, as an unexpected invitation from holy friends into a world he couldn't have imagined—a world in which he *already is somebody*. A somebody with real potential for participating in that inbreaking grace that he's beginning to feel. A somebody with the capacity to envision and embody new possibilities for social innovation.

Mashinini discovered that conjunction of blessing, hope, forgiveness, and friendship in a way that stimulated his imagination with a growing capacity to improvise. He began to see the possibility of God doing miracles in the world, and he was led to provide leadership to others without becoming an obstacle himself.

Ironically, we learn through holy friendships how to envision our own contributions so that we are no longer focused on ourselves. We no longer shrink into that self-absorption that is a mark of sin; rather, we discover life-giving self-forgetfulness that emerges out of a clear sense of our gifts and strengths as well as our blind spots and weaknesses. We become focused increasingly on the larger purposes of God, and in so doing, paradoxically discover our purpose without needing to be preoccupied with ourselves.

Friendship enables us to discover forgiveness, and forgiveness helps us become better and more faithful friends. The forward-looking, life-giving energy that we discover in these relationships are rooted in, and point us toward, a sense of blessing and hope that come to us as a gift from God. And they enable us to dream dreams we otherwise never would have dreamed. And who knows what might happen as a result: a hospital might get built, or a village called Maison Shalom might be developed, or an unjust regime might be overturned.

God's miracles can and do break forth every day. They are more likely to do so when Christians are formed to have character that holds optimism and pessimism together in hope; that recognizes the extraordinary capabilities that we humans have and our capacity for violence and self-destruction; that sees that brokenness can be transformed when it is brought within a context of blessing; that enables us to dream dreams we otherwise wouldn't have dreamed and execute on those dreams. The miracles of Christian social innovation entail human effort, and those efforts are enhanced by practices that shape well-formed character.

The kind of character that grows out of holy friendships offers us a God-centered pattern that transcends and reframes our human tendency toward inconsistent swings between despair and pride. True Christian character resists despair because it finds its foundation not in human effort but in divine initiative; the End of God's reign that reminds us that in the beginning (and the end) is the triumph of God's grace and God's love. Christians participate in that divine initiative, of course, but when personal struggles arise in the process, God's hands stretch out to comfort and guide us. Likewise, true Christian character resists pride because Christians understand just how self-absorbed we can be outside of that grace-filled, divine embrace. Christian character is always God's achievement, done in us, through us, and with us. Christian character, therefore, occupies a space between despair and pride; a space best described as humility.

Recall Moses's situation "in the wilderness." In Numbers 12, we find Moses in a context he's grown used to by this point in Israel's history: conflict. Miriam and Aaron have spoken against him, claiming that he has broken divine teaching by marrying a woman from Ethiopia. They then extend their complaint, asking whether God speaks only to Moses, or to the two of them as well. The third verse in Numbers 12 then interrupts the narrative, inserting a parenthetical remark instead: "(Now the man Moses was very *ʿānāw*, more so than anyone else on the face of the earth.)"

Beyond the general strangeness of such a parenthetical interruption, a particular word looks rather strange. The singular use of the Hebrew word *ʿānāw* appears almost nowhere else in scripture, and in the places where a related term does appear—the plural *ʿănāwîm*—a common translation is "the meek." Yet many translators opt to define *ʿānāw* as "humble" instead, displaying our traditional association between humility and meekness. We tend to tie humility to notions of self-effacement, submissiveness, and a lack of gumption.

In other words, we tend to define humility negatively: knocking someone down off a prideful pedestal, for example. But does the author of verse 3 really want us to imagine Moses as weak-willed, like the awkward kid in the back of the classroom who knows the answer but won't draw attention to himself? Or should we imagine Moses as assertively meek, like the nerdy kid who knows the answer, but gives others a chance to raise their hand before subtly raising his own? Or something else altogether?

Richard Briggs links Moses's humility to his relationship with God. Against Aaron and Miriam's mediated encounter with God, for example, Moses communicates with God "face to face." In this "unique role," according to Briggs, Moses is "directly present before God," and therefore "set apart from all other people." A dependent relationship with God and personal humility are tightly linked: humility "is dependence upon God," Briggs writes, "and, in particular, it is dependence upon God for any speaking of a divinely authorized word."[2]

In this light, verse 3 doesn't look quite so strange. Aaron and Miriam are right to perceive an inequality between themselves and Moses. What they fail to perceive, however, is that such inequality doesn't arise through arbitrary favoritism. God doesn't pick Moses at random; God picks Moses because God *knows* Moses and Moses *knows* God. And a mark of really knowing God is the humility to acknowledge that humans aren't *God* yet are *God-like*. Humble relationship with God, in Moses's terms, straddles these two human realities: we are dependent upon God as finite creatures, and we are also tasked with responsibility for God's finite

---

2. Richard Briggs, *The Virtuous Reader* (Grand Rapids, MI: Baker, 2010), 60.

creation. True humility lowers us below God, and also raises us above much of the created world (see Psalm 8). Indeed, one of the remarkable lessons of Numbers 12 is a counterintuitive one; Moses's humility doesn't make him less active, less assertive, or less convicted. Instead, it makes him *more* active, *more* assertive, and *more* convicted. It makes him a "faithful handler of the word of God," in Briggs's terms. And it makes him, in our terms, an exemplar of traditioned innovation.

It's worth pausing to reflect on what it means, for Moses and for us, to be one of God's humble "handlers." To be a "handler" of something means, in the first place, to have received it from another. Yet the reception is not static; that's "holding."[3] Holders are expected simply to preserve the thing: "Hold my Coke while I run into the store" means "I want my Coke to be in its current shape when you return it."

Handlers, on the other hand, are typically expected to *engage the thing*. We misspeak when we say, "Hold my baby while I run into the store" because we really want that baby *handled*. We see "handle with care" on signs everywhere, because we only handle things of precious value. If our baby gets sick while we're in the store, we want that person to "handle her with care," which verges on redundancy. Handling *means* caring. It means, quite literally, to take something into one's own hands for the sake of fostering intimacy. Even if the baby doesn't get sick, we don't imagine someone passively holding her like a Coke. We imagine them actively handling her by attending to her needs or by trying to make her laugh using an absurd arrangement of silly faces. It's no secret

---

3. I am indebted to Nathan J. Jones for this wonderful image of "holding" and "handling" and for his thoughtful exposition of the contrast.

that those who can make a child laugh earn trust from that child well into the future.

So when Briggs calls Moses a "faithful handler" of God's word, he points to a relationship of trust. God's word is precious, and God trusts Moses because *only humble people can handle* (see also Paul in 1 Cor 15:3). Only humble people know what it means to receive something precious, to get to know it intimately, and to do something faithful and creative with it. Only humble people can suspend their own will in order to pay attention to the will of another thing or person, and only humble people are trusted to do something radically new with something deeply treasured. Traditionalists hold; bearers of a tradition handle. Traditionalists grasp whatever they treasure—the imagined purity of a bygone era, accepted norms of behavior, the "right" way to interpret texts—and hold it close to the vest. They hold it so tightly that they squeeze its life out, leaving it sick, finished, and deflated. Traditionalists' humility is thus one-sided, capable of receiving but incapable of really *responding*. And so it isn't really humility as a virtue but merely the appearance of it.

Attentive, caring response is the domain of tradition, where humility has an active, shaping presence. Humble handlers of tradition still treasure things like cherished pasts, behavioral norms, and interpretive rigor, but the treasure doesn't lie in reception alone. Within a tradition, the treasure lies in being an active participant in its growth, with a posture of cultivation rather than preservation. Traditions, like babies, are living organisms that demand humble handling. And it is only in such handling that we discover, and develop, humility as a virtue.

It is in such handling that we also discover faithful patterns of innovation. Far from being a force of disruption for disruption's sake, traditioned innovation requires the humility to know how to preserve what needs to be preserved so that what is innovated— including, at times, radical innovation—is faithful and life-giving rather than destructive. It requires the virtue of humility; it also requires other virtues, and ultimately aims at the "crown" of virtue: practical wisdom.

Mashinini's courage was cultivated through friendship with human mentors who were focused on God; Moses's humility was cultivated through friendship with God directly. But single virtues only go so far; as Aristotle argued in his *Nicomachean Ethics* (and as Christian thinkers such as Augustine and Aquinas have also shown), virtues must coalesce to form *phronesis*, or "practical wisdom." As a rough definition, think of practical wisdom as the capacity to do the right thing in the right way. It's not the sort of thing that we're born with, or that we can acquire through reading about in a book. It is a finely honed capacity for "thinking-feeling-perceiving-acting" rightly in various situations, and that capacity can only be cultivated and transmitted through experience in intimate human friendships and faithful practices. The practically wise learn to do things "naturally" (as a "second nature"), without having to make difficult decisions, because they have been formed in such wisdom across time.

We need to be formed in practical wisdom if Christian social innovation is to be both faithful and effective. Aristotle conceived of practical wisdom as the crown of the virtues, in large part, because of life's intractable ambiguity. Other virtues, like humility, aim to strike a golden mean somewhere between deficiency and excess, like self-effacement and vanity. Courage moderates between cowardice and bravado, generosity moderates between liberality and greed, and so on and so forth. Even the most humble or courageous people, however, still face the ambiguity of particular situations. What does it mean to be courageous when stepping onto a performance stage, as compared to the courage it takes to step onto a battlefield? Does it take a different form of courage to jump in front of an assassin's bullet? Finding any sort of golden mean in these situations depends upon all sorts of contextual factors: time, place, people involved, and even seemingly minor factors like mood, body language, or the weather.

We can never predict all the various configurations these factors may take, and thus we need practical wisdom to perform *any* virtuous act. Further, we need the virtues taken together, and that is why practical wisdom is an *integrative* way of living holistically and faithfully. In order to be truly humble, we need courage. And in order to be humble and courageous, patience and truthfulness are required. So we learn that in order to cultivate any virtue, we ultimately need them all in their interrelations—and that is a pattern of becoming practically wise.

Practical wisdom treats each context of discernment as a whole, attentive to as many particular dimensions of the situation as possible. Accordingly, practical wisdom requires more than just thinking. It requires feeling out the situation by reading others' emotions in addition to one's own; practically wise people have high "emotional intelligence" quotients and thus express deep empathy with others and their needs. Practical wisdom requires a high level of perception by paying attention to the qualities of people and things present. Eventually, when the various strands come together in a process of discernment, practical wisdom requires careful action. Therefore, practical wisdom is something of an implementing virtue. It takes other virtues—like humility and courage—and implements them into the particular situations that make up our daily lives.

Practical wisdom is essential to Christian social innovation; modern Western Christians have tended to undervalue it because we haven't really talked about it or described its importance. Yet it isn't only an Aristotelian virtue; it is central to what it means to have our lives patterned in Christ and to bear witness to God's reign. It is at the heart of Paul's letter to the Philippians, though we typically don't notice the call to practical wisdom because of many English translations.

Consider a crucial phrase of Paul's in Philippians 2:5: "Let the same mind be in you that was in Christ Jesus" (NRSV). If we read this verse as "mind," we take Paul's exhortation to be primarily an intellectual exercise: as if all we need is to learn about Jesus, study his life and word, and arrive at doctrinal agreements together. Too often we characterize Christians as "believers," as if right convictions held in our brain are all that being Christian involves.

In his Philippians commentary, however, Stephen Fowl argues that much is lost when we constrict Paul's message to the "mind of Christ." Constriction is the issue, too, because the Greek *phronein* carries much richer and multivalent senses than "mind" alone. As Fowl notes, *phronein* comes from *phronesis*, which means that we really should be speaking of an entire manner of thinking, feeling, perceiving, and acting. We should be speaking, in other words, of what it means to embody the practical wisdom of Jesus Christ in our lives and communities.[4]

---

4. The Common English Bible is preferable in its translation of *attitude* ("Adopt the attitude that was in Christ Jesus") rather than *mind,* though it doesn't capture the full context of Paul's argument about character, and it drops the "you" in the second person plural, which might give the impression that this "attitude" is only an individual challenge.

Fowl even suggests that this emphasis on practical wisdom represents "the climax" of Paul's letter, and he names the Christ-hymn in particular (2:5-11) as "one of the most theologically significant passages in the New Testament."[5] Consider what happens to the rest of the passage if we take Fowl's richer conception of Christ's *phronein*. Verse 2 suddenly fits. Paul's joy is made complete by the Philippians "manifesting a common pattern of thinking and acting [*phronein*], having the same love, being bound together by this common way of thinking and acting." Already Paul links the manifestation of communal *phronein* to a sense of common friendship, of "being bound together." And how? By avoiding "selfish ambition and vain conceit," choosing instead to "consider others as your superiors." As Paul concludes this passage with an injunction to attend to the interests of others rather than oneself, an underlying Pauline connection becomes apparent: the bonds of friendship in Christian community are formed through the humble exercise of *phronein*, the practical wisdom of Christ.

This connection emerges even more vividly when we consider what this richer translation of *phronein* does for understanding the Christ-hymn in verses 5-11. Now the focus is not only on Christ's mind, but on his whole manner of thinking, acting, perceiving, and feeling. The focus shifts from Christ's mind to Christ's character, in effect. In this light, verses 6-11 function as a descriptive image of Christ's *phronesis*. It involves thought: Christ "considers" in verse 6. It involves action: Christ "empties" and "takes" in verse 7, "becomes obedient" in verse 8. It involves perception: Christ only empties himself after first perceiving an opportunity to use his divine status as an opportunity for embodying human life. And these thoughts, actions, and perceptions have their source in

---

5. Stephen E. Fowl, *Philippians* (Grand Rapids, MI: Eerdmans, 2005), 89.

character traits like humility and obedience, which Christ "displays" for the church.

Verses 5-11 become a lens for seeing the kind of church Paul yearned for in verses 1-4: a church "bound together" in imitating Christ's pattern of thinking, acting, perceiving, and feeling. Such a church, Paul knew, could nurture intimacy with God and sustain holy friendships with each other. Indeed, in this sense Paul's entire letter to the Philippians is an expression of holy friendship, intended to challenge the Philippians to make Christ's model of *phronesis* apparent in their community. As Fowl puts it, "The structure of this passage reminds us that these are not so much the commands of an officer to troops as the directives of one Christian friend to other Christian friends based on their common vocation to live in a manner worthy of the gospel."[6]

Practical wisdom also shapes Paul's exhortations in Philippians 4:4-9. Verses 4-7 focus on the patterning of our perceptions and emotions, noting that there is a "peace" that surpasses "understanding" and will keep our "hearts and minds in Christ Jesus." Verse 8 focuses on the wisdom that comes from careful thinking and discernment, and verse 9 calls us to habits of behavior that imitate Paul as he has imitated Christ. They all come together in coherent, faithful, virtuous lives redeemed by Christ, shaped by the End of God's reign, and enlivened by the Holy Spirit.

Few would argue with the notion that practical wisdom entails careful thinking and action. Most discussions of social innovation on the one hand, and Christian life on the other, emphasize both thinking and action. Yet we tend to forget just how vital the formation of emotions and perceptions are to *phronesis*, and how dependent we are on holy friends for that formation. We

---

6. Ibid., 78.

forget, for example, that the exercise of practical wisdom always involves particular people and particular situations—*these* people and *this* situation.

Any wise Christian practice, then, entails the ability to perceive a situation rightly and to empathize with the people involved. Perceiving rightly doesn't just mean having functioning faculties, as if a sober mind and clean eyeglasses would do the trick. These faculties clearly matter, but what's really at stake is the ability to perceive what's going on underneath the surface: What kinds of connections do I see between these various things? What kind of history do these things have? Where might God be working through the Holy Spirit here? Inevitably, these perceptive questions will extend to the human actors involved: What kinds of motivations are at play? Who do I know these people *to be*? Who here can I trust?

When these questions arise, we enter the realm of emotional intelligence. The most practically wise Christians pay attention to emotional thermometers, reading mood swings and considering what emotional outbursts or reclusive shyness might signify. As I learned from my daughter Sarah's uncommonly perceptive insights into people's character as a young girl, emotional intelligence can emerge in people well beyond what they might know cognitively or do actively. Emotions don't explain everything, and that's the point: emotions, like thoughts, actions, and perceptions, explain parts of a whole. Only discernments and decisions made in light of the whole can be called practically wise.

Although holy friends are important for the cultivation of any virtue, they are especially crucial for exercising the emotional intelligence and perceptive eye necessary for growth in practical wisdom. When it comes to reading the motivations and emotions of others, guesswork typically fails. The same body language or vocal tone might signify two different emotions in two very different people. We need to really *know* people if we want to read their emotions. Only with intimate friends can we confidently interpret what *that* tone of voice meant, or be able to intuit the presence of an unspoken emotion. Moreover, only intimate friends help us build emotional intelligence, because only they have earned our deepest trust. Only they can challenge us when our emotional life has gone awry, and only they can see the potential for a deeper emotional life. Only a holy friend would see, for example, a potential social worker in the shape of an emotionally distraught drug addict, or the possibilities an angry, embittered person might have to channel those emotions into a vision for innovative ways to address homelessness.

Notice that this holy friend *sees*. The emotions that holy friends feel for each other change their perceptions of each other. Once you feel *for* a friend, you begin to perceive them differently. You now see them refracted through the light of empathy, which shines on them to reveal something divine. Empathy helps friends perceive each other the way God perceives all of us: as vulnerable, broken creatures nevertheless capable of extraordinary faithfulness and innovation. Absent direct address from God, our holy friends' dreams for us are the most powerful way we understand that calling of "who God wants us to be." Holy friends also offer support and sustenance for us, and we for them, as we engage in diverse forms of Christian social innovation. None of that could take place, however, without the empathy and holy perception involved in the exercise of practical wisdom.

We learn to become practically wise through practices and friendships that shape our pattern of thinking, feeling, perceiving, and living. And Paul suggests in Philippians 2:5 that this pattern is to be the same that was in Christ Jesus. Practical wisdom is learned and lived in the presence of the crucified and risen Christ, empowered by the Holy Spirit who is making all things new by conforming us to Christ. And it is learned and lived in community as a lifelong project, as the Wesleyan movement at its best has emphasized.

Holy friendships encourage traditioned innovation by nurturing practical wisdom; they also help us to be storytellers. We learn practical wisdom in part by telling our own (and our friends') stories in life-giving ways in the light of God's reign. Holy friendships cultivate shared practices that enable us to recognize the interconnected character of our stories and to reframe and re-narrate our lives into God's story.

In *Redirect: The Surprising New Science of Psychological Change,* Timothy Wilson calls this approach to learning how to reframe our and others' stories "story editing," and he reports numerous social science studies that show the significance of such an approach. Wilson writes that story-editing techniques share three assumptions:

- We must see the world through others' eyes if we want to change behavior;
- Our interpretations are not always set in stone and can be redirected; and
- Small changes in interpretations can have self-sustaining effects that create long-lasting behavioral changes.[7]

Holy friends help us discover storytelling skills by reorienting us to God, to God's blessing, forgiveness, and love in Christ, and

---

7. Timothy D. Wilson, *Redirect* (New York: Little, Brown, and Company, 2011), 238.

to the power of the Holy Spirit who is making all things—including you and me—new. They redirect our perspectives, and reframe things so we can see life afresh—and can thus be set free for faithful and effective social innovation.

Cultivating a Christian Vision for Today

What practices nurture holy friendships that help us learn to reframe and edit our stories, to be formed into people shaped by the End and who practice traditioned innovation? Key practices that support and sustain holy friendships are found throughout the New Testament, and as we saw in chapter 2 especially in the book of Acts: they include listening, reading (scripture and other resources), crossing borders, praying, worshipping, practicing silence, and breaking bread.

At the center of these practices is the commitment to create time and safe spaces in which faithful, and faith-filled, story editing can occur. **Listening is a key practice that continually focuses our attention beyond ourselves.** How often do we really listen to those to whom we are speaking? Without discipline, our minds return to the past and jump to the future, missing out on the present. Faithful listening builds the trust that enables acquaintances to come to know each other more deeply. This practice requires discipline to set aside time on a regular basis to really hear a friend's stories, and to do so with our hearts focused on how God's Holy Spirit is working in and through them.

Study and learning, through reading widely and "crossing borders" (especially by engaging others who think differently from us), opens our hearts, minds, and whole beings to others and reminds us that God-centered friendship draws us all into communion with each other. It deepens our commitment to learning throughout life (see chapter 2). Studying scripture in a way that forms a scriptural imagination shapes our lives as disciples of Christ and connects us to those who have walked in the way of the Light before us; it helps us locate our stories in the larger context of God's story. Reading across disciplines exposes us to new ideas and ways of thinking, makes connections across sectors, and shows us the many ways God is present.

Likewise, crossing borders, embedding ourselves in new places and with new people, sets our sights on the abundant diversity of the places, cultures, and people of our world. It puts us in touch with the challenges we face today, and it directs us toward contexts where hope is flourishing. Broadway United Methodist Church in Indianapolis experienced revitalization in part because they appointed a staff person whose title was "roving listener," responsible primarily to be out in the community around the church and to pay attention to the diverse community that now lived in their neighborhood. Through this intentional listening, they discovered some painful things (e.g., how unwelcoming the church felt to many neighbors), some shared interests (e.g., different people interested in a community garden or in the arts), and some new ideas for social innovation (e.g., incredibly talented cooks were able to begin catering businesses).

Praying, worshipping, and practicing silence are communal and solitary practices that focus us in responsive attentiveness to God and God's reign. Through these practices we intentionally listen to God, speak to God, and give thanks to God. Often some of our best story-editing insights are discovered through these forms of relationship with God. These practices have been central to the shaping of Maggy's imagination and to sustaining her in her leadership. So also has been the Eucharist for Maggy; she discovers in the pattern of "take, bless, break, and give" an attentiveness to Christ's redeeming work that also reminds her that our brokenness is covered by God's blessing. **Sharing a meal, or breaking bread, is a fundamental act of our life together as Christians.** Preparing food and sharing it signals our care and nurture of another person. This act invites us into deeper discernment about showing hospitality to strangers and recalls the ways that Jesus invited all people to the table. There is a deep connection between sharing stories and breaking bread, reflected in the Gospel narratives, as well as in the lore of families and lifelong friends.

Taken together, this story-editing approach and the practices that undergird it enable us to connect with other people on the deepest of levels, sharing our fears and failures, our hopes and dreams. Wilson notes that "the best predictor of happiness is the quality of our social relationships."[8] He goes on to say that, even so, our perspective on the world can be shaped to make us happier. The key? Having a story about ourselves that gives us meaning, hope, and purpose.

Holy friends help us edit the stories we are used to telling about ourselves: challenging sins, affirming gifts, dreaming dreams. Wilson's story-editing techniques can be practiced by individuals; they include reflecting on upsetting events as though a distant observer, imagining our future lives and then writing down what it would take to get there, and doing good works that connect us to others and our best selves.

Yet we are most likely to engage in such activities if we are part of larger communities of holy friends who accompany us to

8. Ibid., 49.

see the truth of our lives in the complex interconnections of sins, gifts, and dreams. They help us discover answers to the "why"; through these relationships, we discover a sense of purpose for the world, for our lives, and we are inspired and empowered to engage in transformational social innovation.

Forming communities and institutions that nurture holy friendships help us learn practical wisdom and practice Christian social innovation. The practices described in chapters 1 and 2 point us to the centrality of cultivating communities and new institutions that both embody Christian social innovation themselves and lead to other forms of Christian social innovation. In our day, this involves both reforming and renewing existing communities and institutions *and* forming new ones.

Dreaming for Transformation

New and renewed patterns of learning practical wisdom through small groups have emerged in recent decades as practices of traditioned innovation. For example, the Disciple Bible study program, begun in the late 1980s through the leadership and vision of Dick and Julia Wilke, had a powerful impact in many congregations. In nearly thirty years, hundreds of thousands of people began a journey of Christian discipleship through these small groups, and started to cultivate a scriptural imagination through study and friendship. This program even took on forms of Christian social innovation as, for example, when the Disciple program was introduced into prisons and enabled new patterns of engaging prisoners and exploring prison reform. A Youth Disciple was also developed to engage a younger generation.

The Disciple program has also stirred the imagination of lay Christians to undertake new experiments in social innovation, sometimes with extraordinary impact. For example, a layperson in the First United Methodist Church of Coral Gables, Florida, Alvah Chapman, had his imagination stirred as his Disciple class moved through the story of scripture. When they focused on Matthew 25, things began to click for Chapman, and he felt called to explore a new vision for dealing with homelessness and poverty.

Chapman was an influential person in Miami, the retired chairman and CEO of the Knight-Ridder Corporation. Inspired by his newfound Christian imagination, and nurtured by others in his Disciple group, Chapman began a series of conversations with influential leaders in Miami. The result was the formation of a Community Partnership for Homelessness, a project in social innovation that cultivated a public-private partnership for housing and support to help formerly homeless people become self-sufficient. It became a model for other communities across the country—and it all started in a Christian community reading the Bible together.

More recently, new patterns of church planting and other forms of "fresh expressions" are cultivating Christian communities that help people begin to learn practical wisdom. Whether gatherings focus on the longing for faithful relationship in covenant (as in the successor to Disciple, Covenant Bible Study) or are occurring over dinners (as with Alpha, which began in the Church of England), or in coffee shops or on running trails, the key is to develop a fellowship in which people begin to explore the wisdom of God in relationship together.

A Christian community called the Refuge, and its associated business Coffee Oasis, is a powerful Wesleyan fresh expression of the gospel located in Bremerton, Washington. Both Refuge and Coffee Oasis are oriented toward reaching, nurturing, and discipling what they describe as "street-oriented youth." The Refuge is the Christian community that gathers for worship, study, and fellowship. Coffee Oasis is a business and place of hospitality; it provides financial resources that help to sustain the ministry, and it is also integrally connected to the vision of the ministry and their commitment to formation. Their vision is "Christ. Healing. Community." As they describe their vision more fully on their website,

A church of the city.
Incarnating King Jesus in city life.
Speaking its language.
Singing its rhythms.
Sharing spaces.
Freeing the oppressed.
Fighting injustice.
Finding people of peace.
Inviting the city into the Kingdom of God.

Anyone and everyone is welcome in the community, especially teenagers who feel like they have no home and nowhere else to go. Coffee Oasis welcomes them into the community and engages in deep, creative patterns of learning in order to focus them on the End. They are committed to traditioned innovation, and in their larger vision they are exemplary practitioners of Christian social innovation. They are inviting the whole city to both see and participate in the End that is God's kingdom.

Such innovation can also occur in rural communities that might seem more challenging contexts. This is as true of rural

North Carolina as it is of rural Burundi. A rural congregation in an impoverished area of eastern North Carolina, Calvary Memorial United Methodist Church, saw a need and opportunity to engage the community in learning and formation in a digital age. The congregation developed a learning opportunity focused on using computers. And, in a twist appropriate to social innovation but unusual in a congregation, young people are the instructors for a mostly older population. The initiative is providing energy for renewal in the congregation, the surrounding county, and support for economic development more broadly.[9] Their engagement has drawn people who would not otherwise have known of the congregation into new patterns of relationship with the church and each other.

These new initiatives combine a welcoming environment for people with opportunities to go deeper in their formation through intimate gatherings. The "holy friendships" described in this chapter are especially analogous to the Wesleyan movement's "bands," those groups that gather in more intimate ways for accountability, support, and transformation. As we move from being seekers to being disciples, we will long for more intensive patterns of formation. We need intimate gatherings that will deepen our habits and practices and offer the challenge, affirmation, and invitation to dream that will enable greater faithfulness, new life, and transformational social innovation.

In addition to creating patterns that welcome people, as well as intimate gatherings that help people go deeper, we also need to focus on the wider ecosystem that nurtures Christian formation. At its best, Christian social innovation depends on intrinsic

---

9. See "Plugged In…to the Future," *Faith & Leadership*, April 12, 2010, https://www.faithandleadership.com/features/articles/plugged-the-future.

partnerships of diverse institutions that support the formation of a broad Christian vision and help people discover and learn practical wisdom. Those institutions include schools, camps, publishing houses, health clinics, retirement homes, initiatives to help children (and adults) learn marketable skills that become sustainable, coffee shops, entrepreneurial businesses, and varieties of skunkworks incubating new innovations.

This wider ecosystem will depend on "keystone" institutions that are responsible for ensuring the newly created institutions continue to see themselves as intrinsically related to each other and to existing ones. Keystone institutions are organizations of sufficient scale, scope, and influence that their leadership shapes the entire ecology beyond their own internal purpose. Apart from the leadership role of keystone institutions, we too often settle into silos where institutions see themselves as essentially separate from each other and devolve into extrinsic relationships that are largely based on survival and contractual exchanges of goods and services. Rather than life-giving innovation through collaboration, institutions tend to devolve into a self-destructive blame game.

A healthy ecosystem for learning practical wisdom will cultivate a form of "institutional holy friendships." The institutions themselves will learn to challenge the sins each other has come to love, to affirm gifts each other has been afraid to claim, and dream dreams they otherwise wouldn't have dreamed. The Florida Conference of the United Methodist Church began cultivating these relationships more intentionally, recognizing that their Fresh Expressions project is deeply connected to their congregations, to their Warren Willis Camp, to the campus ministries of their colleges, and to new patterns of social innovation where they can overinvest in young people.

At this point, you may be wondering. The previous chapter ended with a powerful story of a woman, Maggy Barankitse, and this one began with a remarkable story about a young man, Tsietsi Mashinini. But now I have been talking about communities, institutions, and even an ecosystem of institutions. Is Christian social innovation about these amazing, transformative individuals? Or is it about teamwork, communities, institutions, and ecosystems?

The answer is both. Here, as elsewhere, we need to think "opposably" rather than "either/or." Unfortunately, we are used to thinking in oppositional terms, and even to telling our stories as mutually exclusive. Is it all about the creative visionary, or is it all about the community and the team? We have a tendency either to glorify the individual, and downplay, if not outright ignore, the importance of all those people who enable social innovation to be sustained and even scale. Or we swing the pendulum the other way and argue that the real work of leadership and innovation is found in teamwork; individuals don't matter that much, if at all.

Yet transformational social innovation does depend to a significant extent on brilliant visionaries and amazingly creative innovators who see systems and strategies and possibilities that many of the rest of us cannot see. And the genuinely brilliant have a gift that transcends even ordinary vision. If it is said that the talented can accomplish things the rest of us can't quite reach, the truly transformational geniuses envision things we haven't even imagined. Their vision and practical wisdom are of a different order than ours.

We ought to celebrate such brilliance, creativity, and wisdom whenever we encounter it *and*—here is where we need to be opposable rather than oppositional—we also need to honor and recognize the communities that helped form them to flourish and continued to support and sustain them in their work. The now clichéd phrase "it takes a village to raise a child" is nonetheless true, and it takes a village to practice Christian social innovation.

Even as the brilliant innovators seek to cultivate new ecosystems of intrinsic partnerships as they develop innovative approaches, they need wise people who help to sustain those partnerships themselves. Not everyone needs to be a creative, visionary social innovator; but we do need everyone to share in a commitment to the importance of ongoing renewal and innovation for the sake of faithful witness to the gospel. Many, perhaps most, will happily be parts of teams, doing a lot of the quiet work that is essential to sustaining communities and institutions—and to renewing them.

When we have experienced the effects of a narcissistic innovator whose self-absorption, self-aggrandizement, and selfish ambition cause wreckage in relationships and even in the innovative work itself, we often react by focusing only on the health of the community. We have seen the destructive effects of what Iris Murdoch called "the fat, relentless ego." And so we want people to give up their egos, or at least we ask them to "check their egos at the door."

Mike Krzyzewski is the Duke basketball coach who has also been the head coach of the USA Men's National basketball team for the past twelve years. He realized in forming a team of NBA stars—people like LeBron James, Kobe Bryant, and Kevin Durant—to be on the Olympic team, it wouldn't work to ask them to get rid of their egos, or even to check them at the door. Rather, he told them that he wanted them to "bring their best ego, their best self, to the service of the team and their larger mission to represent the USA and win a gold medal."[10]

Coach K was articulating a principle that has an analogy in biblical wisdom. Paul enjoins the Philippians (in the NRSV translation), "Do nothing from selfish ambition" (2:3). The adjective *selfish* here suggests there is a form of ambition that is appropriate for followers of Jesus: an ambition for God's reign. Too often we think we need to put away all ambition when we see the destructiveness of selfish ambition, when we are really called to bring our highest ambition, our best egos, to the service of an extraordinary purpose and mission: God's reign.

The dreams holy friends help us dream, and that we help them dream, are cultivating such ambition. They challenge us to put away our self-absorption, and they affirm gifts we may not have seen, in order that transformational witness and social innovation might be developed. Regardless of whether the result is a small-scale innovation in a local community or institution, or the kind of large-scale transformation characteristic of a new hospital system in Indiana, an ecosystem for orphaned children in rural Burundi, or a vision for a new South Africa, we are called to bear witness to the Holy Spirit who is making all things new. We are invited, and expected, to let love make us inventors.

10. Coach K described this to the author in a personal conversation.

A CHILD'S BLESSING

The love that makes us inventors, that shapes a Christian vision of social innovation, is nurtured at the intersections of six themes: blessing, hope, friendship, forgiveness, imagination, and improvisation. Living at these intersections enables us to learn and relearn, to discover and rediscover, the power of the Holy Spirit who is making all things new.

Throughout this book I also emphasized that a Christian vision for social innovation needs to invest deeply in young people, even "overinvest" in them, for their passion and enthusiasm will help us dream big and to imagine things we might not otherwise have imagined. Such was the case with the youth that launched Indiana's Methodist Hospital, with the children who have helped to imagine and scale Maison Shalom, and with Mashinini's vision of a new South Africa.

Young people will surprise us in large and small ways. A young child offered a blessing to his mother that provides an image to guide the renewal of Wesleyan witness. It was a blessing that itself reflects a mindset of traditioned innovation, connecting deeply to the Christian tradition with an innovative way of pointing to the work of the Holy Spirit.

117

The young child was our son Ben, when he was nine years old. One night, shortly after my wife Susan had tucked him into bed and given him a kiss goodnight, Ben pulled her back toward him and then kissed her on the forehead, four times down and three times across. He then said to her, "Mom, you are blessed."

Susan was surprised and moved. As she realized what he had done, she said, "Ben, do you realize that you kissed me in the form of the cross?"

"Yep," he said, "I planned it that way."

Wiping a tear from her eyes, Susan said, "Thanks, Ben. You are blessed, too."

Susan and I eventually realized that Ben had had two recent experiences in which someone had made the sign of the cross on his forehead. Earlier that year, during a service of renewing our baptism, the pastor had taken water, marked the sign of the cross on Ben's forehead, and said, "Remember your baptism, and be thankful." A couple of months later, on Ash Wednesday, the pastor had taken ashes, marked the sign of the cross on Ben's forehead, and said, "Repent, and believe in the gospel."

With the creative imagination of a child, Ben had improvised on the tradition and offered a blessing to his mother. It was a blessing that connected forgiveness and friendship, and focused on the hope that is at the heart of a Christian vision for social innovation. It is a blessing that encourages all of us to bear witness to the Holy Spirit's work in conforming us to Christ: to offer kisses in the form of the cross.

CPSIA information can be obtained
at www.ICGtesting.com
Printed in the USA
LVOW01s2255310316

481661LV00002B/2/P